CLASSROOM GUIDANCE

FROM

A TO Z

26 Ready-To-Use Lessons For Grades 5-9

By
Becky Kirby

ABOUT THE AUTHOR

Becky Fesemyer Kirby has been an educator for 37 years, and a school counselor for the past 19 years. Becky works with seventh- and eighth-grade students at Brown Middle School in Ravenna, Ohio. In 2008, Becky was selected as one of the semi-finalists for *American School Counselor Association's Counselor of the Year.*

Becky received an B.S. degree in education from Kent State University. She received a master's degree in school counseling from the same university.

Becky lives in Ravenna with her husband David. Their three children, Kristine, Greg, and Jeff, are all graduates of Ohio State University.

Becky is the author of *Grab Bag Guidance* and *Ways To Amaze and Engage Middle School Students,* published by Mar*co Products, inc.

CLASSROOM GUIDANCE FROM A TO Z

10-DIGIT ISBN: 1-57543-147-5   13-DIGIT ISBN: 978-1-57543-147-5

GRAPHIC DESIGN: Cameon Funk
COVER PHOTOGRAPH: © Creatas • Images, School Days, 15429-26AT

REPRINTED 2010
COPYRIGHT © 2007 MAR*CO PRODUCTS, INC.
        PUBLISHED BY MAR*CO PRODUCTS, INC.
        1443 Old York Road
        Warminster, PA 18974
        1-800-448-2197
        www.marcoproducts.com

DEDICATION

I dedicate this book to my granddaughter, Maggie Mei Ratliff. Maggie was born in Changsha, Hunan, China, and joined our family on August 8, 2005. She is the daughter of Kristine and Charles Ratliff and is one of the joy of our lives!

I also dedicate this book to all of my wonderful Kent State University practicum students: Emily Brinkman, Stacy Bubenzer, Brian Carr, Carmella Labriola, Johanna Pionke, and Margaret Van Fossen. They have encouraged and supported me and they have given me ideas and suggestions to make this book the best it can be. I appreciate each one of them!

TABLE OF CONTENTS

INTRODUCTION

Classroom Guidance From A To Z was developed because of the need to address specific subject areas in middle school. Teachers often ask me, as the counselor, to present a lesson on a specific problem they are dealing with in their classroom. Because I have no lesson plans to follow, I often have to make up lessons. So you won't have to reinvent the wheel, this book contains specific, easy-to-follow directions on how to teach lessons on a variety of topics.

The lessons are varied and versatile, fun and effective. Easy to present, they require few materials and, for the most part, rely on student participation. Each lesson teaches a life skill and follows one of the three domains of student development in the American School Counselors Association (ASCA) National Model: *academic development, career development,* and *personal/social development.* The ASCA Standards for each lesson are found at the beginning of the lesson.

Each lesson should take approximately 45 minutes to present. The facilitator can alter activities to shorten or lengthen some lessons. Since I think it is important to have a surplus, rather than a deficit, of information or activities, the lessons are designed to easily take up an entire 45-minute period.

School counselors will find these activities helpful, and classroom teachers will also find them beneficial. This book can be used to teach lessons during advisor/advisee sessions in school that offer such programs. Mental health is an important component of health education, and health teachers may find worthwhile lessons in this book. Club advisors, camp counselors, and group facilitators may also find ways to incorporate these lessons when working with youth.

I hope that you find these lessons easy to use, motivational, and beneficial for your students. Enjoy!

Becky Kirby

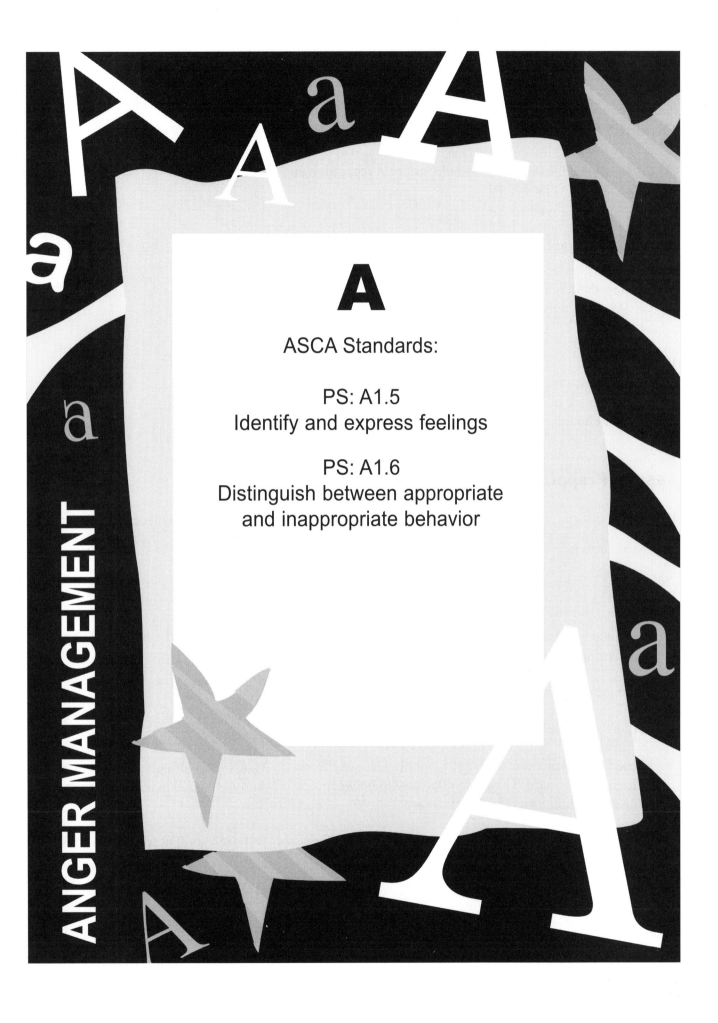

A

ASCA Standards:

PS: A1.5
Identify and express feelings

PS: A1.6
Distinguish between appropriate
and inappropriate behavior

ANGER MANAGEMENT

ANGER MANAGEMENT

Objective:

To dispel myths about anger and help students recognize anger cues and anger triggers and learn healthy ways to express anger

Materials Needed:

For each student:
- ☐ 10 sticky notes
- ☐ Pencil

For the leader:
- ☐ *Anger Myth Cards* (pages 14-15)
- ☐ Cardstock or heavyweight paper
- ☐ Chalkboard and chalk or whiteboard and marker

Lesson Preparation:

Reproduce the *Anger Myth Cards* on cardstock or heavyweight paper. Gather the necessary materials.

Lesson:

▸ Introduce the lesson by telling the students that they are going to talk about the feeling of anger and learn to identify anger triggers and healthy ways to handle anger.

▸ Write the word *ANGER* on the board.

▸ Tell the students that *anger* is a normal, healthy feeling.

▸ Show the students that *ANGER* is one letter away from *DANGER* by adding a *D* to the word written on the board. The close relationship between *ANGER* and *DANGER* makes it necessary to discuss healthy ways to handle anger.

▸ Divide the students into two groups. Distribute sticky notes. Tell each student to take 10 sticky notes.

- ▸ Divide the board into two areas.

  - • Label the first area *Anger Cues*—How do you know when you are getting angry or when someone else is getting angry?
  - • Label the second area *Anger Triggers*—What are some of the things (triggers) that make people angry?

- ▸ Tell the students that the first group will write answers to the question about anger cues and the second group will write answers for anger triggers. Each student is to write a separate answer on seven of his/her sticky notes, then put each sticky note on the board under the correct topic. *(Note: The remaining three sticky notes are used later in the session.)*

  - • *Anger Cues* could include: rapid heartbeat, increased body temperature/red face, tense body, mean look, clenched jaw, stomachache, sweating, etc.
  - • *Anger Triggers* could include: being called names, insulting my family, being pushed, being talked about, having your things taken, being ridiculed, etc.

- ▸ Discuss what the students have written, noting that some answers may correctly appear in both categories.

- ▸ Point out that it is important for the students to be aware of anger cues and of what triggers angry feelings in themselves or in someone else.

- ▸ On the board, write:

  When I am angry, I …

- ▸ Discuss anger-reducing techniques and other healthy ways to handle anger.

- ▸ Ask each of the students to write three things he/she does when angry. The students should use a separate sticky note for each thing and, when finished, stick the notes on the board. *(Note: As leader, feel free to add your thoughts.)*

- ▸ There are three rules for handling anger in a healthy way:

  - • Rule One: You may not hurt yourself.
  - • Rule Two: You may not hurt anyone else.
  - • Rule Three: You may not destroy property.

- ▸ Have the students take turns removing sticky notes that name actions that are hurtful or destructive. Put these notes to one side. *(The notes removed typically refer to: hitting, kicking, punching, yelling at someone, slamming things, throwing things, swearing, using drugs/alcohol, blowing up at people, locking up anger, and leaving. The students may not think that leaving is hurtful, but it can be if someone leaves without telling anyone where he/she is going and when he/she will be back.)*

▶ Notes describing healthy ways of handling anger may be left on the board. Some of these answers could be: *going to my room, journaling, exercising, listening to or playing music, watching or playing sports, crying, talking with someone, thinking about something else or changing the way I think about whatever happened to make me angry, relaxing, taking a bubble bath, and playing videogames.* These are healthy ways of dealing with anger in an indirect manner.

▶ If a person chooses to deal with anger in a direct way, it is important not to use direct confrontation. Your expression of your anger can be heard if you:

- Are calm—talk to yourself, saying things like *stop, stay calm,* and *think*
- Pick the right time

Use non-blaming behavior, such as an "I" statement. An example of an "I" statement is: "When someone calls me a name, I feel angry because I don't like to be put down." Identify the behavior, describe how you feel and the reason you feel that way, but do not blame anyone for making you feel that way. Sometimes just identifying the behavior and the way you feel is all you have to do. That means just saying something like: "I feel mad when someone calls me a name." Forming "I" statements takes practice, and we will practice them shortly.

▶ When confronting someone who makes you angry, it is important that you:

- Not jump to conclusions
- Not bring up the past *(Let go and move on.)*
- Not use words like *always* and *never*
- Not be demanding
- Realize you may have to negotiate
- Try to find a common ground, such as mutual concern about a situation
- Understand that you and the other person may have to *agree to disagree* and that it is OK to do that

▶ Write the formula for an "I" statement on the board.

When (<u>STATE THE BEHAVIOR</u>), I feel (<u>FEELING WORD</u>), because (<u>REASON</u>).

▶ Ask for volunteers to role-play the use of "I" statements. Emphasize that the volunteers are to follow the formula on the board, but that they need not necessarily put the phrases in the same order.

▶ First role-play:

- A boy in your class keeps throwing wads of paper at you. *(Possible statement: "When things are thrown at me, I feel angry, because it disrupts me and those around me.")*

▶ Second role-play:

- Your friend lost your homework, which was inside a book he borrowed from you. *(Possible statement: "I feel upset when I let someone borrow something I need and then it is lost.")*

▶ Third role-play:

- Your teacher never calls on you. *(Possible statement: "I think what I have to say is valuable, so I feel left out when I raise my hand but never get to answer.")*

▶ Ask the students to suggest other situations and make "I" statements regarding those situations.

▶ Ask for seven volunteers to each read an anger myth to the class. Give each volunteer a card with a myth written on it. After each myth has been read, have the students who are not volunteers explain why the statement is a myth. After a short time, have the student holding the card read the italicized answer. Then have the next volunteer read the myth on his/her card.

Anger myths:

- We all have the same emotional makeup. *(Of course, everyone is different. We all come from different backgrounds and we have learned different messages about anger.)*
- Anger always results in aggression. *(Anger can be expressed in a non-blaming way, without aggression.)*
- Venting anger is always the best thing to do. *(Not necessarily. If you don't pick the right time, if you blame someone for something, if you raise your voice, there could be consequences.)*
- Nice girls don't get angry. *(Everyone gets angry. Anger is a normal, healthy feeling, and it is not healthy to keep feelings locked up.)*
- It is not OK to feel angry. *(Feelings are not good or bad. What we do with our feelings is what matters. It is OK to feel angry.)*
- We might lose control and go crazy if we show we are angry. *(This will not happen if you use the correct steps for showing anger.)*
- We have to get even with people who are angry with us. *(It is never OK to get even with someone.)*

▶ Ask the students who are not volunteers if they can think of any other myths about anger.

Conclusion:

▶ Conclude the lesson by reviewing anger cues, anger triggers, healthy ways to handle anger, and myths about anger.

We all have the same emotional makeup.

(Of course, everyone is different. We all come from different backgrounds and we have learned different messages about anger.)

Anger always results in aggression.

(Anger can be expressed in a non-blaming way, without aggression.)

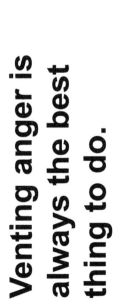

Venting anger is always the best thing to do.

(Not necessarily. If you don't pick the right time, if you blame someone for something, if you raise your voice, there could be consequences.)

Nice girls don't get angry.

(Everyone gets angry. Anger is a normal, healthy feeling, and it is not healthy to keep feelings locked up.)

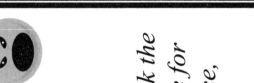

14

We have to get even with people who are angry with us.

(It is never OK to get even with someone.)

It is not OK to feel angry.

(Feelings are not good or bad. What we do with our feelings is what matters. It is OK to feel angry.)

We might lose control and go crazy if we show we are angry.

(This will not happen if you use the correct steps for showing anger.)

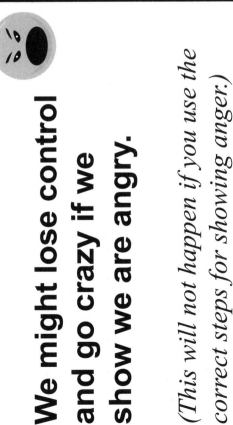

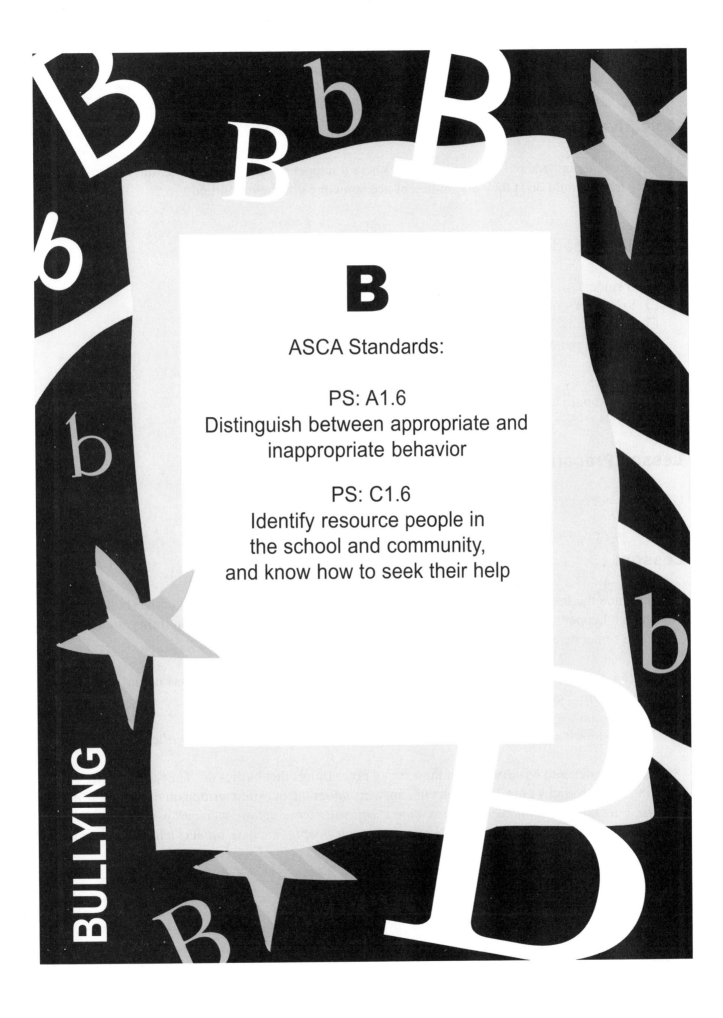

B

ASCA Standards:

PS: A1.6
Distinguish between appropriate and
inappropriate behavior

PS: C1.6
Identify resource people in
the school and community,
and know how to seek their help

BULLYING

BULLYING

Objective:

To help students understand what bullying is, where it happens, why some people bully others, and what students should do if they are bullied or see someone else being bullied

Materials Needed:

For each student:
- ☐ 8-10 sticky notes
- ☐ Pencil
- ☐ Piece of paper

For the leader:
- ☐ Chalkboard and chalk or whiteboard and marker

Lesson Preparation:

Gather the necessary materials. On the board, write: *What is bullying?*

Lesson:

▸ Introduce the lesson by telling the students that they are going to talk about what bullying is, where it happens, why some people bully others, and what students should do if they are bullied or see someone else being bullied.

▸ Ask the students to answer the question *What is bullying?* Record their answers on the board and discuss them. Point out that bullying is harassment.

▸ Distribute 8-10 sticky notes to each student. On the board, write: *What do bullies do?*

▸ Tell the students to write on half of their sticky notes things that bullies do. They are to write one thing on each sticky note, then stick their answers under the question written on the board. *(They will write things like: take your lunch money, call you names, ignore you, call your mom names, take your things, talk about you, throw things, hit people, exclude others, trip people, make people feel scared, etc.)*

CLASSROOM GUIDANCE FROM A TO Z © 2007 MAR∗CO PRODUCTS, INC. 1-800-448-2197

- On three separate places on the board, write:

  - Physical bullying
  - Verbal bullying
  - Emotional bullying

- Read the answer on each sticky note and call on individual students to move each note into the correct column (physical, verbal, or emotional). Discuss each example and why it belongs in a specific category.

- On another part of the board, write: *Where does bullying happen?*

- Have the students write one answer on each remaining sticky note, then stick the finished notes on the board. Review what the students have written. *(They will write things like: locker room, cafeteria, hallways, bus stop, on the way to and from school, classroom, etc.)*

- Tell the students that it is not their job to hit, trip, nudge, call names, or hurt another person. It is not their job to isolate, humiliate, and/or exclude others. If they are doing any of these things and/or using other forms of harassment, they are bullying. Let them know that if these things are happening to them, they are being bullied.

- Emphasize that the person being bullied is not responsible for the bullying.

- Ask the students why someone would bully another person. *(The may say that bullies feel insecure, bullying makes some people feel powerful, bullies have low self-esteem, bullies have problems at home, bullies think bullying makes them look good, bullies like to show off, etc.)*

- Make it clear that any student behaving in this way needs to ask him/herself:

  - Why do I feel I need to put someone down or hurt someone?
  - What is going on with me?
  - Am I a bully because someone has bullied me?
  - What do I need to work on?

- Tell the students that anyone who thinks he/she is bullying should talk with a counselor or a trusted adult.

- Explain that people who feel good about themselves do not put others down. At this point, you may want to ask the students whom they know who never bullies anyone in any way.

- Ask the students to describe what they can do if someone bullies them.

- Make sure the students understand that if they are being bullied, even if they walk away or yell "stop," they must talk with an adult about what has happened. Emphasize that the rule is: **Report, report, report**. Explain that anyone who is a victim of bullying must report what has happened to an adult. Reporting bullying is not tattling. It is being assertive. When you report bullying, you are sticking up for yourself, sending the message that no one is going to treat you like that.

19

▶ Ask the students:

- What can you do if you see someone being bullied?
- What are some reasons a person who saw someone being bullied might not try to stop what was happening?
- Why would bystanders go along with the bully, and do something like laugh while they watched someone being bullied?

▶ It is often difficult for students to stop bullying, whether it is happening to them or to someone else. Remind the students that it is best for them to report bullying to an adult and to let the adult handle the situation. Emphasize again that reporting bullying is not tattling. It is being assertive, sticking up for themselves and/or for someone else. Encourage the students to trust the adult to do the right thing.

▶ Emphasize that bullies should never be encouraged and that bullying should never be ignored.

▶ Ask if the students have any questions or if there is anything they would like to discuss in more detail.

Conclusion:

▶ Conclude the lesson by telling the students that bullying must be stopped and that we must work together to provide a safe environment for all of us. Tell the students to take out a piece of paper and write a sentence stating one way they will help put a stop to bullying. Tell them to keep their statement and look at it from time to time to make sure they are doing what they said they would do.

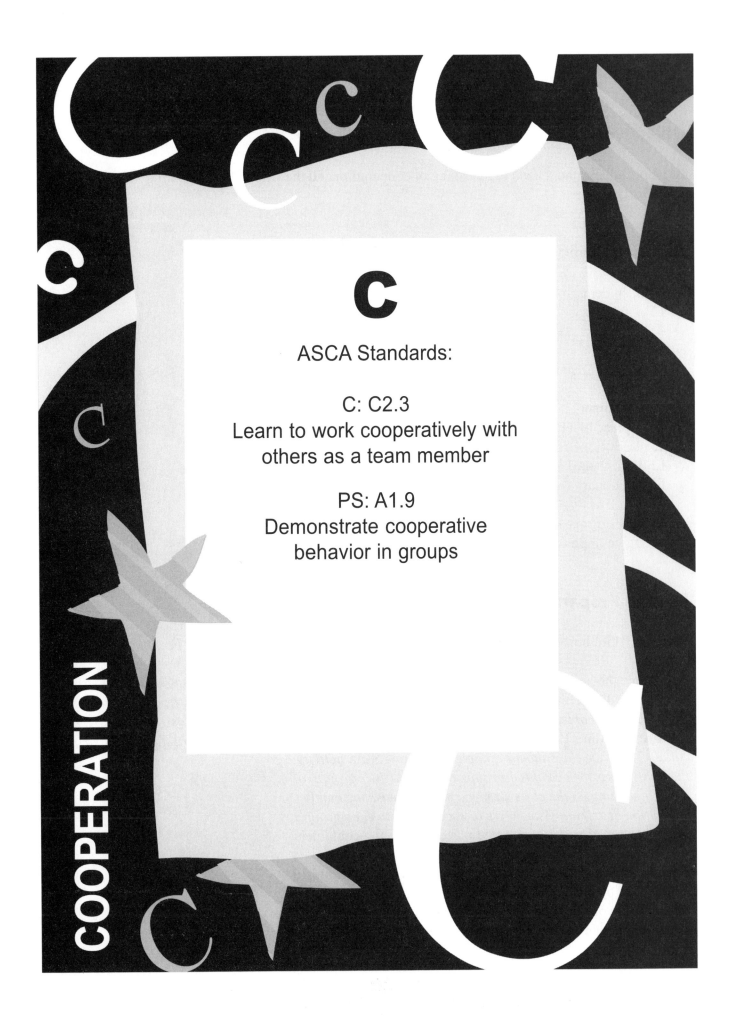

C

ASCA Standards:

C: C2.3
Learn to work cooperatively with others as a team member

PS: A1.9
Demonstrate cooperative behavior in groups

COOPERATION

COOPERATION

Objective:

To help students understand the meaning of cooperation and the value of participating in a cooperative effort

Materials Needed:

For each student group:
- ☐ 1 fresh egg

For the leader:
- ☐ 1 *Song Strip* for each student in the class (page 26)
- ☐ Scissors
- ☐ Container
- ☐ 1 piece of 11" x 16" tagboard for each group in the class
- ☐ 1 envelope for each piece of tagboard
- ☐ Chalkboard and chalk or whiteboard and marker
- ☐ Dictionary (optional)
- ☐ Stack of 8½" x 11" white copy paper
- ☐ Rolls of masking tape
- ☐ Table or desk

Lesson Preparation:

Optional: Hard boil the eggs. *(Note: Do not let the students know the eggs have been hard-boiled.)*

Reproduce the appropriate number of *Song Strips* (one for each student in the class). Cut the strips apart, then divide them into equal or nearly equal sets. *(For example: If you have 28 students, Reproduce six copies of page 26. This will give you six of each of the five song strips [30 strips]. Remove one* Mary Had A Little Lamb *strip and one* Jingle Bell *strip, so the total number of strips equals 28. When the students complete the* Song Strip *activity, they will have formed three groups of six and two groups of five. Depending on the class size, you may decrease the number of sets you distribute. Assign five or six students to each group.)* Fold the slips of paper in half and place them in the container.

Cut the 11" x 16" pieces of tagboard into five or six puzzle pieces. The number of puzzle pieces should match the number of students you plan to have in each group. Place the puzzle pieces into an envelope.

Place the white copy paper and masking tape on a table or desk.

On the board, write *COOPERATION*. Gather any other necessary materials.

Lesson:

▸ Introduce the lesson by asking the students the meaning of the word *cooperation*. *(They will give such answers as: working together, helping each other out, and sharing responsibilities.)* Read a dictionary definition of the word or recite the following dictionary definition:

Cooperation: the act of working together for a common purpose.

▸ Ask the students to name times when they must cooperate. *(They may say things like: playing sports, in class, working on a project, etc.)*

▸ Ask the students to point out some of the advantages of group cooperation. *(They may say that when they cooperate with other members of a group: they accomplish more, achieve a better result, have fun, find it satisfying, etc.)*

▸ Tell the students that for the remainder of the period, they will be forming groups and will participate in activities that require them to cooperate with the other members of the group.

▸ Have each student draw a *Song Strip* from the container. The students may not show anyone the song title on the paper they have selected.

▸ Tell the students to begin humming the song on their paper and walk around the room to find others who are humming the same song. When a student finds someone else humming the same song, these students are to stand together.

▸ Once the students have formed groups of others humming the same song, tell them they are going to begin the first group-cooperation activity.

▸ Give each group a puzzle. Tell the students that each of them is to take a puzzle piece from the envelope. *(Note: If the number of pieces in an envelope is greater than the number of students in the group, have some students take two pieces.)* Each group is to put its puzzle together. Group members may not talk while completing the task. Tell the groups how much time they have to complete this task.

▸ When the allotted time has elapsed, ask the students:

• How did the members of your group work together?
• How did you communicate with other members of your group?
• Did one member of your group take charge, become the leader? If so, how was this person chosen?

- How did the members of your group help each other?
- What feelings did you have? Did you feel frustrated?
- Is there a group that did not complete the puzzle? If your group did not put the puzzle together, why didn't your group complete the task?

▶ Remind the students that in order to complete this activity, they had to cooperate with the other members of their groups. Explain that this activity included:

- A Goal—What was the goal?
- Awareness—What were you aware of?
- Trust—What role did trust play in this activity?
- Challenges—What were some of the challenges to completing this activity in the allotted time?

Tell the students that working with others involves goals, awareness, trust, and challenges.

▶ Explain that when working on a group project, it is helpful to begin by brainstorming ideas. It is important that group members listen to each other and provide feedback to each other. When each member of the group cooperates, everyone will learn more and the project will be more fun. Every member of a group is expected to participate in a group project. Some roles are helpful when students are working together to reach a goal. The group benefits if group members take roles for which they are best suited. The roles are as follows:

- Recorder—takes notes
- Reporter—lets everyone know what the group is doing, has done, and plans to do
- Cheerleader—encourages everyone to participate, shares ideas, and gives feedback
- Facilitator—keeps the group on task
- Observer—keeps an eye out for group members who need to be more involved, keeps track of who participates

▶ For the next activity, have the students remain in the same groups. Ask the group members to take a few minutes to choose their roles in their respective groups. Explain that this activity also requires group members to cooperate with one another. This time, though, they may talk.

▶ Show the students the materials available for the activity: white 8½" x 11" copy paper and masking tape.

▶ Give each group a fresh egg. Tell the students their group is to make a contraption that will hold the egg. The invention must stand by itself, holding the egg in place. Tell the students they will have 15 minutes to complete this task.

▶ Instruct the students to begin brainstorming, get their materials, and get busy.

▶ When the allotted time has elapsed, have each reporter describe his/her group's finished product. Ask each reporter:

- Did every member of the group participate?
- Who took charge in your group?
- What problems did your group encounter?
- What limitations did your group have?
- How did your group get organized?
- What worked?
- What didn't work?

▶ Ask the students what happens when someone doesn't cooperate or doesn't do his/her share of the work. *(They may say that someone who does not cooperate on a group project can: cause bad feelings, resentment, and frustration because others have to do more work.)*

Conclusion:

▶ Conclude the lesson by reminding the students that cooperation is a matter of give and take. Cooperation allows everyone to contribute his/her special talents to create a better product or outcome. People can accomplish more when they cooperate, and cooperation can make any task more satisfying and more fun.

SONG STRIPS

Mary Had A Little Lamb

Jingle Bells

Old MacDonald Had A Farm

Twinkle, Twinkle Little Star

The Farmer In The Dell

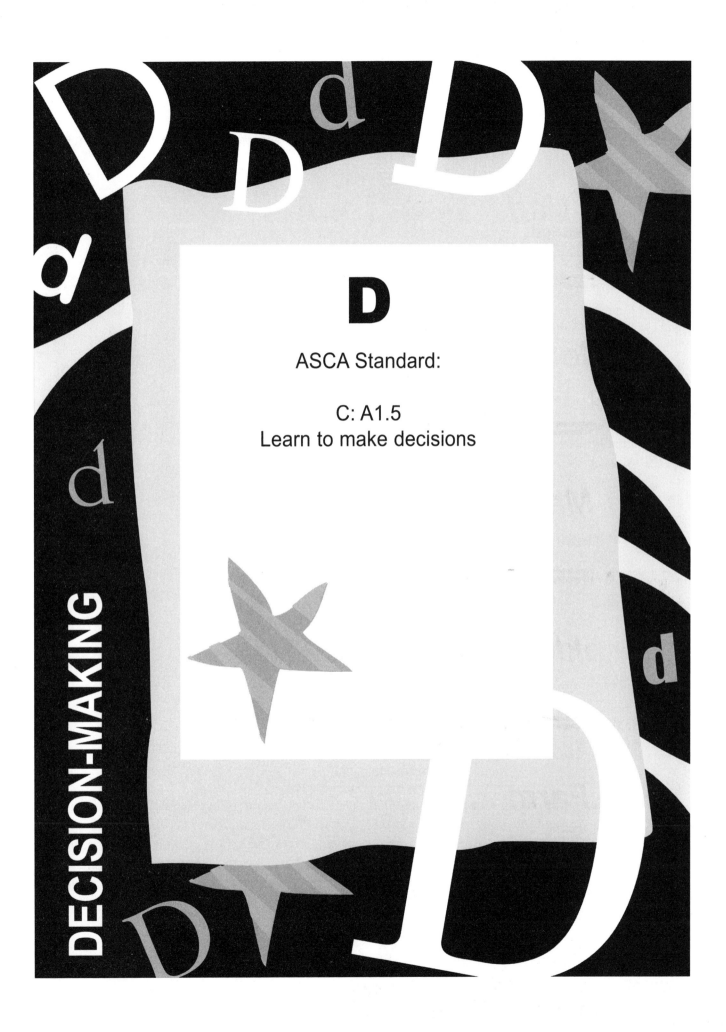

D

ASCA Standard:

C: A1.5
Learn to make decisions

DECISION-MAKING

DECISION-MAKING

Objective:

To learn the five steps for making a decision and strategies for making the best decision

Materials Needed:

For each student:
- ☐ 8-10 sticky notes
- ☐ Pencil
- ☐ Piece of paper

For the leader:
- ☐ 1 *Animal Strip* for each student in the class (page 32)
- ☐ Scissors
- ☐ Container
- ☐ Posterboard
- ☐ Marker
- ☐ *Decision-Making Situation Cards* (page 33-34)

Lesson Preparation:

Mark the posterboard as shown:

THE 5 C'S OF DECISION-MAKING

Clarify the problem
Consider the options
Compare
Choose
Carry out

After you carry out your decision,
always evaluate to determine whether
you made the best decision.

Reproduce the appropriate number of *Animal Strips* (one for each student in the class). Cut the strips apart, then divide them into equal sets. *(For example: If you have 28 students, Reproduce six copies of page 32. This will give you six of each of the five animal strips [30 strips]. Remove one bird strip and one snake strip, so the total number of strips equals 28. When the students complete the* Animal Strip *activity, they will have formed three groups of six and two groups of five. Depending on the class size, you may decrease the number of sets you distribute. Assign five or six students to each group.)* Fold the slips of paper in half and place them in the container.

Reproduce the *Decision-Making Situation Cards*. Cut the cards apart.

Lesson:

▸ Introduce the lesson by telling the students that they are going to talk about different kinds of decisions and learn a technique that will help them make the best decisions.

▸ Ask the students to take out a pencil and a piece of paper. On the paper, tell each student to list all the decisions he/she made the day before. Tell the students to begin with deciding to get up, what to wear, etc. Give the students enough time to complete the task.

▸ Explain that decisions can be categorized as *automatic, daily, or major.*

- *Automatic decisions* are just that—automatic. They involve things we do without much thought. An example of an automatic decision is getting up in the morning.
- *Daily decisions* are decisions that we make every day. Some examples of daily decisions are brushing your teeth and eating breakfast.
- *Major decisions* require us to weigh pros and cons and look at options in order to make the best decision each time. These decisions often affect our values and goals. Some examples of major decisions are choosing a college or whether to start smoking.

▸ Tell the students to look at what they have written and to mark an *A* next to every *automatic decision*, a *D* next to every *daily decision,* and an *M* next to any *major decision* listed. When everyone has finished, ask the students to tell the class about any *automatic decisions* they have listed. Then invite them to describe any *daily decisions* listed. Then ask them to identify any *major decisions* they made previously.

▸ Tell the students the formula for making good decisions. Position *The Five C's Of Decision-Making* chart so everyone can see it.

▸ Pointing to each *C,* review its meaning with the students.

- Clarify the problem—make its meaning clear
- Consider options—look at other ways to solve the problem
- Compare all the options
- Choose the best option
- Carry out the plan to make the best decision

Emphasize that once a decision has been made, it is important to evaluate the consequences in order to determine if it was the best decision that could have been made.

▸ Have each student draw an *Animal Strip* from the container. Tell the students not to tell anyone the animal's name on the paper they have selected. Explain that they will form groups according to the animal name on each person's paper. Each student is to make the sound made by the animal whose name is written on the paper he/she chose and walk around the room, listening to find others who are making the same sound. All those students who are making the same sound will form a group.

▶ Give each group a *Decision-Making Situation Card*. Explain that the groups may refer to *The Five C's Of Decision-Making* chart to help them determine which decision is best. Each group will need to choose a reporter to tell the class about the group's situation and the decision the group members have made. Tell the students they have 10 minutes to complete this activity.

▶ Reinforce the following strategies for making the best decision:

- Know what is important to you.
- Think about what you know about yourself and what you've learned from decisions you and others have made in the past.
- Consider all your options and check to see if any of these options entail any risks.
- Once you make a decision, you must accept any consequences of the choice you have made.
- Evaluate every decision you make.

▶ **Optional Activity:** While the students are still in their groups, ask them to make a group decision for each of the situations below. Each reporter will then tell the rest of the class what decision his/her group made.

Scenario #1—On Saturday, you and your friends must go to one of these places together:

- the movie theater
- glow-in-the-dark miniature golf course
- the shopping mall
- game room and restaurant

Scenario #2—You and your friends have a chance to earn money by working together to:

- baby-sit a group of 5-year-olds
- mow lawns
- wash cars
- deliver flyers to houses

Scenario #3—Your group has won a trip. Where will you decide to go?

- New York City
- Orlando, Florida
- NASCAR races
- Hollywood, California

Scenario #4—You and your friends must all order the same drink. What will it be?

- Root beer
- Chocolate milkshake
- Strawberry smoothie
- Cola

Scenario #5—You may choose one place to go Friday night. Where will you choose to go?

- Movies
- Concert
- Arcade
- Party with your group and other friends

▸ Ask the group if these decisions were hard to make. If some group members disagreed with the rest of the group, have them describe how the disagreement was resolved and how the group arrived at its final decision.

▸ **Alternate Activity:** Using the previous questions, designate areas in the room where the student groups are to gather according to the answer they choose.

Conclusion:

▸ Conclude the lesson by reviewing *The 5 C's Of Decision-Making* and reinforcing the importance of making good decisions.

ANIMAL STRIPS

Dog

Elephant

Lion

Snake

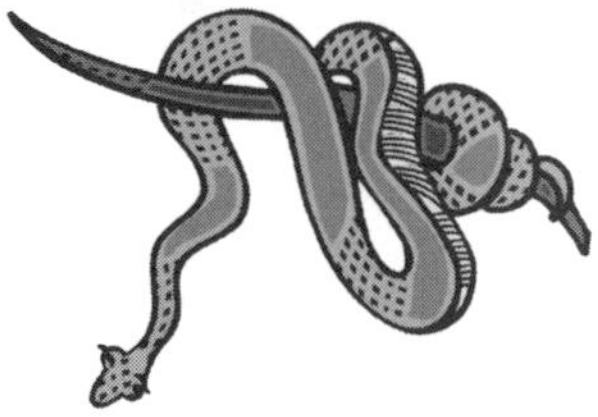

Bird

You told your friend you would go to the movies with him/her on Friday night. Your cousin has invited you to come and watch him/her play in the championship basketball game. You really have wanted to see this game.

What will you decide to do?

Your teacher received $100.00 in grant money for your class. The money may be spent on anything that has to do with science that you will study this school year. Your teacher has chosen you to be the chairperson of a committee to decide what to buy.

How will you decide what to buy?

You have been chosen to attend a three-day camp with students from area schools. You are looking forward to going and meeting new friends. You just found out that your school dance will be held on the Friday you leave for camp. Your school holds only two dances a year.

What will you decide to do?

After P.E. class, you discover the chain you wore to school is missing from your locker. You had taken it off and left it in your unlocked locker. Two days later, you see a student in the hall wearing a chain just like yours.

What will you decide to do?

DECISION-MAKING SITUATION CARDS

You go to a friend's overnight party. His friends from the school he used to attend are there, too. You had never met these friends before, but soon become friendly with them. In the middle of the night, they want to leave the party and walk around town.

What will you do?

You find a $20 bill in the grocery store. You need $20.00 to pay your basketball tournament entry fee.

What will you decide to do?

Your friends want you to go with them to another friend's house after school. This friend's parents will not be home and you think alcohol will be available at the house.

What will you decide to do?

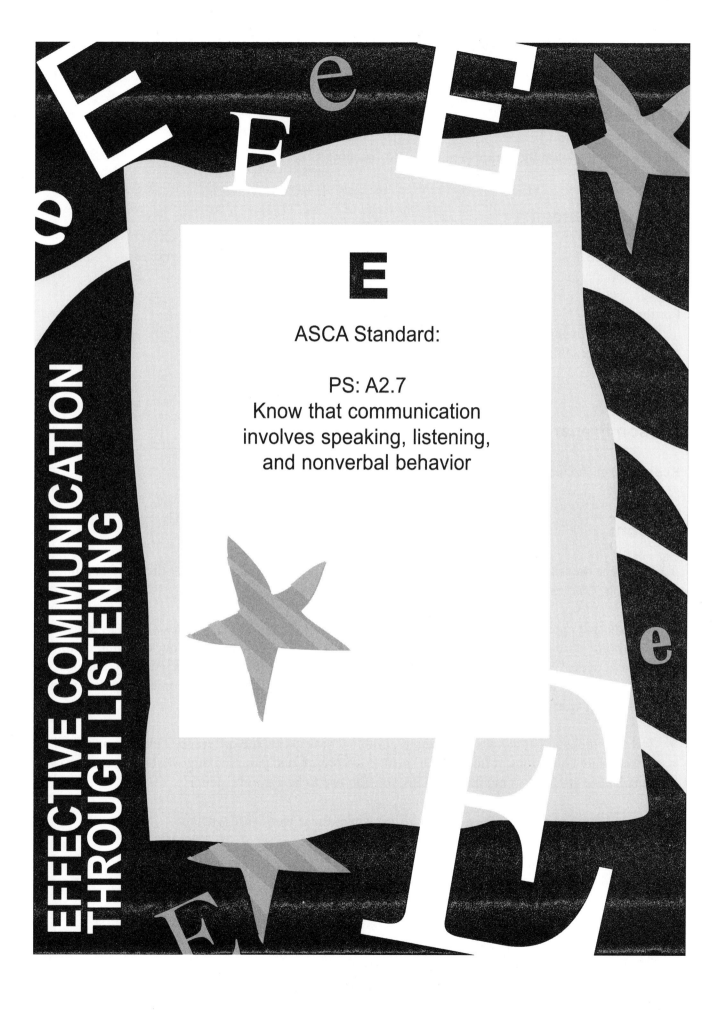

E

EFFECTIVE COMMUNICATION
THROUGH LISTENING

E

ASCA Standard:

PS: A2.7
Know that communication
involves speaking, listening,
and nonverbal behavior

EFFECTIVE COMMUNICATION THROUGH LISTENING

Objective:

To help students learn the components of good listening skills and how to apply them

Materials Needed:

For each student:
    None

For the leader:
- ☐ *Good Communication Cards* (pages 40-42)
- ☐ 3 pieces of different-colored cardstock
- ☐ Timer

Lesson Preparation:

Reproduce each *Good Communication Card* on a different color of cardstock.

Lesson:

▸ Introduce the lesson by asking the students what they think of when they hear the word communication. *(They may say: talking, writing, sign language, listening, etc.)*

▸ Explain that *communication* is *the interchange of thoughts, opinions, or information by speaking, writing, signing, etc.* Communication can help build self-confidence. Your communication is also a part of how you treat others. An important part of communication is listening, and how well you listen is an indication of how well you treat others. Listening to someone makes that person feel worthwhile.

▸ Tell the students that this lesson is about good listening skills, the difference between open and closed-ended questions, reflecting the speaker's feelings, and paraphrasing what the speaker has said. These are all communication skills you can use to be a good listener.

▸ Display the *Good Communication Cards* on which these words are written:

- • Focus
- • Accept
- • Give Feedback

▸ Hold up the card with *Focus* written on it. Tell the students that a good listener will focus on the person who is speaking. Ask the students how a person's body shows that he/she is listening. *(They may say that when a person is listening to someone, the listener's eyes look at the speaker, body is turned toward the speaker, shoulders face the speaker, the listener may lean forward, etc.)*

Continue by explaining that these postures are types of body language. Point out to the students that focusing is paying attention to the speaker. A focused listener can reflect the speaker's feelings by paying attention to how the speaker looks, to the sound of his/her voice, and/or to what the speaker is saying.

▸ Hold up the card with *Accept* written on it. Ask the students what accept means in the context of listening. *(They may say that to accept means: not talking when the speaker is talking, listening even if you disagree with what the speaker is saying, paying attention to how the speaker is feeling, etc.)*

Ask the students how they might show acceptance. *(They might say they could show acceptance by: nodding their heads, smiling, saying uh uh, etc.)*

▸ Hold up the card with *Give Feedback* written on it. Ask the students what giving feedback means. *(They might say giving feedback means: talking back to the speaker, staying on the speaker's subject, paraphrasing what the speaker has said, etc.)* After the listener identifies how the speaker is feeling, he/she can give feedback by paraphrasing what the speaker has said. An example of giving feedback is: *You sound excited that you got the part in the school play.* This is also the time when a listener may express agreement or disagreement with what the speaker has said, ask questions, or give relevant information to the speaker. When giving feedback, the listener must stay on the subject at all times.

▸ Using the following activity, encourage the students to practice the techniques you have just presented.

Have the students form a circle within a circle, with half of the students forming an inside circle and the other half making an outside circle. Each student in the inside circle should be facing a student in the outside circle.

Assign a topic to the students. The students in the outside circle will talk on the assigned topic for as long as one minute. Then the student on the inside who is facing the student gives the speaker feedback for 30 seconds. When you say, "Switch," the students reverse roles, with the students who have given feedback speaking on the same topic for as long as a minute. Throughout this activity, all students are to practice focusing, accepting, and giving feedback.

When it is time to discuss the next topic, each student on the outside circle will take one step to the left, so he/she is facing the next student on the inside circle. Do the same thing with each new topic, with the students on the outside taking one step to the left and the students on the inside circle not moving at all.

▶ Suggested topics are:

- What is your favorite holiday and why?
- Describe a time when you were frightened.
- If you were given $500.00, what would you do with it?
- What do you do for fun?

▶ Tell the students that asking an open-ended question or making an open-ended statement is a good way to get someone to talk when you are listening. An open-ended question or statement requires more than a yes or no answer. Questions that require the speaker to give only a one-word answer are called *closed questions.* Tell the students that people who ask an open-ended question or make an open-ended statement get a lot more information than those who ask closed questions. Choose volunteers to answer the following sample questions:

- (open) Tell me about your school.
- (closed) What school do you attend?
- (open) What is your school like?
- (closed) Do you like your school?

Ask the students if they can hear the difference in the students' answers. Explain that listeners learned a lot more from the open-ended statement or question than from the closed questions.

▶ Ask the students to give other examples of open-ended statements or questions.

▶ Two more effective-listening techniques that are a part of giving feedback are: reflecting the speaker's feelings and paraphrasing what the speaker has said. *(If necessary, define paraphrasing: Paraphrasing is a close restatement of another person's words using your own sentences, often to clarify meaning.)*

▶ Divide the students into pairs. Designate one student in each pair to be the listener and the other to be the speaker. Remind the listeners to use the good-listening skills of focusing, accepting, and giving feedback. Tell each pair of students to choose one of the following topics and discuss it for three minutes:

- Tell about your family.
- What did you do last weekend?
- Who would you like to meet and why?

▶ After three minutes have elapsed, direct the students to select a different topic and reverse roles with their partners.

▶ When each pair of students has discussed a topic, ask the following questions:

- What did you like about listening and not talking?
- Was it hard to give feedback?

- Did anyone reflect the speaker's feelings, and/or paraphrase what the speaker had said?
- Did you feel your partner listened when you were speaking?
- How did it feel to have someone listen to you?

Conclusion:

▶ Conclude the lesson by reviewing the good-listening skills of focusing, accepting, and giving feedback. Ask the students to use these skills to pay attention to what a speaker is saying and to watch to see if others use these good-listening skills. Emphasize that listening is an integral part of communication and that people feel worthwhile when they know someone is listening to them.

FOCUS

41

GIVE FEEDBACK

42

F

ASCA Standard:

PS: A1.5
Identify and express feelings

FEELINGS

FEELINGS

Objective:

To help students learn to recognize personal feelings and to expand students' feeling-word vocabularies

Materials Needed:

For each student:
- ☐ *Feeling Word Grid* (page 47)
- ☐ 2-3 sticky notes
- ☐ Pencil

For the leader:
- ☐ Index cards
- ☐ Marker
- ☐ Table
- ☐ Chalkboard and chalk or whiteboard and marker

Lesson Preparation:

Write a different feeling word on each index card. Suggested words are: *happy, sad, angry, mad, exhausted, calm, miserable, joyful, excited, bored, confident, proud, confused, annoyed, frustrated, frightened, disappointed, hurt, relaxed, interested, puzzled, discouraged, motivated, ecstatic, ordinary, down,* and *hopeful.* Make duplicate cards for any feeling words you choose. Place the cards face-up on a table.

If you are using the *Feeling Word Grid,* make a copy of it for each student.

Lesson:

▸ As the students come into the room, ask them to pick a card that describes how they are feeling.

▸ Introduce the lesson by telling the students they are going to talk about feelings or emotions. Invite the students to explain why they chose the feeling card they did, reminding the other students that feelings are neither good nor bad.

▶ Tell the students that young people often have a hard time talking about their feelings. Then ask:

- Why are feelings so hard to talk about?
- Adolescents feel more emotions than ever before in their lives and their feelings may change frequently in a short period of time. Can anyone describe a time when your feelings changed quickly from one feeling to another?

▶ Then say:

Emotions can make you feel wonderful. They can also make you feel miserable. There are no bad feelings. Any feeling you have is acceptable and OK. It is important to let others know how you feel, accept your feelings, and deal with them in a positive way.

▶ Discuss the ways that people discern how others are feeling and have students volunteer examples. The students may demonstrate some examples of discerning different feelings. These examples could include:

- By the way a person looks (body language)
- By the sound of a person's voice
- By what the person is saying

All of these ways allow us to discern how someone is feeling.

▶ Let the students know that people often use the basic feeling words—*happy, mad, sad*—to describe how they are feeling. Write the words *Happy, Mad,* and *Sad* on the board. Write each of these words at the head of a column.

▶ Tell the students they are going to expand their vocabulary of feeling words so they can use the correct word to express the way they are really feeling.

▶ Divide the class into thirds. Give each student 2-3 sticky notes. The students in the first third of the room are to think of feeling words that mean *happy.* Tell each of the students to write one word on each sticky note and stick the note in the *Happy* column on the board.

▶ The students in the second third of the room should do the same thing with the word *mad.* Those in the final third of the room should do the same thing with the word *sad.*

▶ Tell the students to begin the activity.

▸ When all the students have finished, review the words they suggested. Add any words you or the students think of.

Possible words are:

HAPPY	MAD	SAD
ecstatic	angry	miserable
joyful	mixed-up	upset
calm	envious	lonely
relaxed	annoyed	confused
confident	aggressive	down
interested	disappointed	depressed
eager	frustrated	melancholy
proud	disgusted	left out
optimistic	discouraged	hurt
satisfied	hostile	pained
excited	negative	exhausted
blissful	furious	regretful

▸ Distribute a copy of the *Feeling Word Grid* to each student. Ask the students to choose 16 of the feeling words on the sticky notes on the board and write one of those words in each box on their activity sheet.

Take the sticky notes off the board and place them face-down on the table. Select one of the sticky notes and read aloud the feeling word written on it. The students who wrote that word on their paper may cross it off. Have each student crossing off a word give an example of a time when a person may feel the way that word describes. Continue to follow this format until someone has crossed out four feeling words in a horizontal, vertical, or diagonal row. *(You may also use four corners.)*

Conclusion:

▸ Conclude the lesson by telling the students to be aware of how they are feeling and to use feeling words to express their emotions. Remind them that they should also pay attention to how others are feeling, by listening to them and by observing their body language.

FEELING
WORD GRID

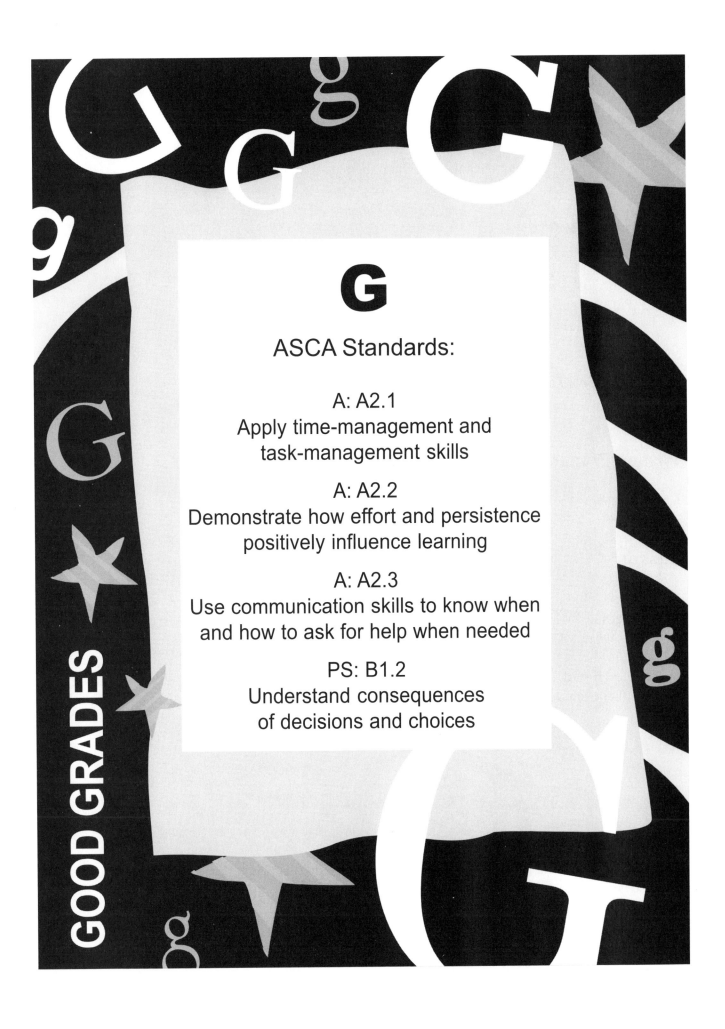

G

ASCA Standards:

A: A2.1
Apply time-management and
task-management skills

A: A2.2
Demonstrate how effort and persistence
positively influence learning

A: A2.3
Use communication skills to know when
and how to ask for help when needed

PS: B1.2
Understand consequences
of decisions and choices

GOOD GRADES

GOOD GRADES

Objective:

To help students learn techniques that will help them earn better grades

Materials Needed:

For each student:
- ☐ *How To Earn Good Grades* (page 53)
- ☐ Piece of paper
- ☐ Pencil

For the leader:
- ☐ Chalkboard and chalk or whiteboard and marker
- ☐ Die

Lesson Preparation:

Reproduce *How To Earn Good Grades* for each student. Gather the necessary materials.

Lesson:

▸ Introduce the lesson by asking the students to brainstorm things they can do in order to earn good grades. Write their answers on the board. *(They will probably say they can do things like: do the work, study hard, ask questions, attend school every day, etc.)*

▸ Give each student a copy of *How To Earn Good Grades*. Tell the students that you are going to give them some tips for getting good grades. Write the letters GRADES on the board like this:

G
R
A
D
E
S

Explain that for each letter, you will give them a tip that will, if followed, help them get good grades.

▶ Let the students know that *G* stands for *Good Attendance*. Then ask:

> How does attendance affect grades? *(When you do not attend class, you miss information, miss assignments, do not complete in-class work, may miss a quiz or test, etc.)*

Ask the students if anyone in the class has had perfect attendance. Commend those students who raise their hands to indicate that they have not missed a single day of school. Allow those students to share their feelings about the importance of coming to school each day.

Emphasize that if a student is absent from school, it is important for him/her to get missed assignments, notes, etc., and make up the work as soon as possible.

▶ Tell the students that *R* stands for *Ready And Prepared For Class Each Day*. Ask the students to discuss what they do to get ready and prepare for class each day. *(They may say they: put their work in folders, trapper keepers, or some other place where they can find it easily; make sure they have the necessary supplies; use a planner to write down assignments and check each assignment off when they have completed it; etc.)*

Reinforce the idea that it is helpful to have everything organized at home and set out for school the night before. Students who do this are not likely to forget assignments, supplies, money, etc.

▶ *A* stands for *Assignments*. It is very important for students to complete assignments on time and turn them in when they are due. In order to accomplish this, students need to:

- Keep track of due dates
- Ask questions if they do not understand an assignment
- Put their finished work in a place where they will be able to find it easily
- Manage their time wisely, so they do not have to rush to complete an assignment
- Turn in their homework

Some students complete their homework, but don't turn it in. Ask the students why someone would do the assigned homework but not turn it in. *(They might say the person: couldn't find the homework, forgot it at home, has a control issue and may be rebelling against a parent, etc.)* If someone mentions a student not handing in his/her homework as a way to rebel against a parent, point out that it is the student, not the parent, who suffers the consequences of this behavior.

▶ *D* stands for *Develop A Plan*. Ask if the students have a plan to help them succeed. Explain that this does not have to be things they have written down. The plan may be things the students know they have to do in order to be successful. Have the students share their plans with the class.

▶ With the students, review the following tips that can be part of their plan to succeed:

- Establish a time and place to study. If your teacher sets aside class time to use for studying, it is important to use that time for that purpose. Study halls are good places for studying, and the adults who monitor study halls can help with any questions you may have. Take advantage of any available after-school tutoring sessions and choose a quiet place and time at home where you can study each day.

- In the classroom, sit where you can see and hear the teacher.
- Don't be afraid to ask questions. If school is out for the day or for vacation, ask an adult or call a friend who may know the answer to your question.
- Take good notes.
- Don't wait until the night before to study for tests.
- Be organized—use a planner, folders, etc.

▶ *E* stands for *Envision Being Successful.* Tell the students to picture themselves earning good grades and to describe that experience. Tell them that a positive, *I Can* attitude can play a part in helping them earn good grades.

Have the students take out paper and pencil and write down a class and the highest grade they think they can earn in that class. You may want to ask them to do this for all of their classes. When everyone has finished, let the students know that they can achieve the grade(s) they have written down if they take the necessary steps to strive to get that grade. These steps include good attendance, preparing for class, completing and turning in assignments, and developing a plan. Most important of all, they must truly believe they can do it.

▶ The last letter in the formula for earning good grades is *S.* It stands for *Study Smart.* Give the students the following smart-studying tips:

- Don't waste your time.
- Get right to the task.
- Review the notes.
- Have someone quiz you on the material.
- Ask questions about anything you don't understand.

Some tricks that you can use to help you study are:

- To recall the words in a list, think of a word that begins with the first letter of each word in the list.
- Make up a sentence that includes each word in a list of things you want to remember.
- Group things you want to remember into categories.

Conclusion:

▶ Conclude the lesson by reviewing the concepts you and the students have discussed. Ask for volunteers to roll one die. Let the volunteers know that they are to tell one thing they learned about getting good grades for each mark on the die they roll.

HOW TO EARN GOOD GRADES

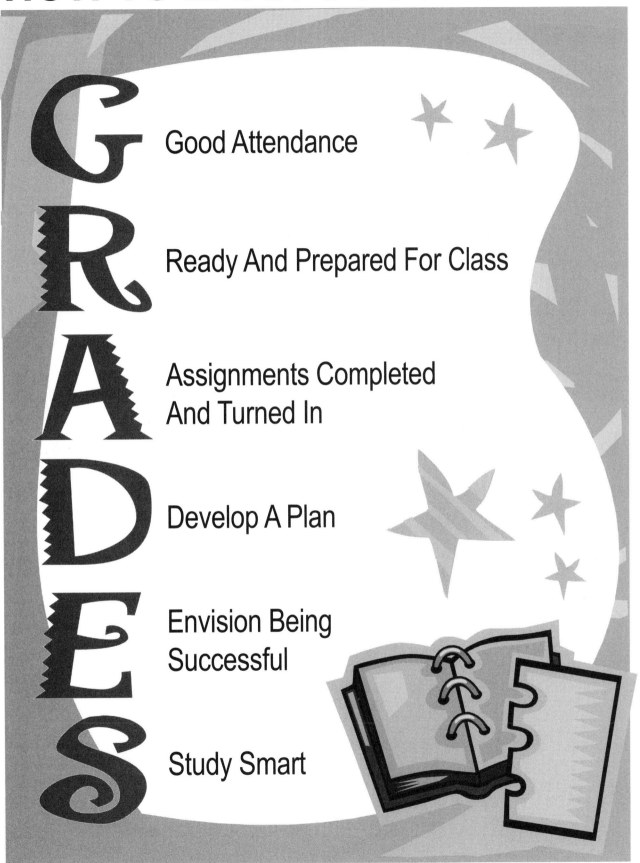

G Good Attendance

R Ready And Prepared For Class

A Assignments Completed And Turned In

D Develop A Plan

E Envision Being Successful

S Study Smart

H

ASCA Standards:

A: A3.4
Demonstrate dependability,
productivity, and initiative

A: B1.3
Apply the study skills necessary for
academic success at each level

HOMEWORK

HOMEWORK

Objective:

To help students learn the importance of doing homework

Materials Needed:

For each student:
- ☐ *Desktop* (page 59)
- ☐ *Homework Bingo—Four In A Row* (page 60)
- ☐ Pencil

For the leader:
- ☐ *Homework Bingo Numbers* (page 61)
- ☐ Scissors
- ☐ Container

Lesson Preparation:

Reproduce *Desktop* and *Homework Bingo—Four In A Row* for each student. Reproduce and cut apart the *Homework Bingo Numbers.* Put the numbers into a container.

Lesson:

▶ Give each student a copy of *Desktop*. Ask the students to visualize all the materials and supplies they need to have at home in order to do homework. Have them write or draw on the worksheet the things they visualize. When everyone has finished the activity, have the students share their ideas with the rest of the class. *(Some things they may mention are: paper, pens, pencils, erasers, folders, paper clips, stapler and staples, ruler, compass, protractor, pencil sharpener, crayons, markers, glue, scissors, sticky notes, correction fluid, highlighters, index cards, books, and assignments.)* Explain that having supplies readily available is an important key to completing homework successfully.

▶ Discuss the advantages of homework, why homework is important, how the students should approach their assignments, and what they should do if they aren't in class when an assignment is made.

Advantages And Importance Of Homework:

Homework is a very important part of being a student and the way you do your homework is an indication of how successful you will be in school. Students who set high standards, and who have clear expectations about how they approach homework, do very well in school. Studies show that students who do their homework perform better on achievement tests than students who do not do their homework. In other words, the more time you spend on something, the better you do.

Homework teaches the lifelong skills of:

- Responsibility
- Self-discipline
- Good study habits
- Time management

It is important to know that you can do homework even if you do not have to turn in an assignment. You can study notes, read, review materials, etc.

How To Approach Homework:

It is good to set aside a certain time to do homework every day. It is also important to make a schedule that includes your other activities. The average time spent on homework is 10 minutes per grade level. If this is the case, how much time should you spend on homework each day? *(7th grade = 70 minutes; 8th grade = 80 minutes, etc.)*

Have the students discuss how they prepare for homework before they leave school for the afternoon. Be sure they mention:

- Making sure assignments are written in a planner that they will take home
- Taking home the books, worksheets, and supplies they will need
- Making sure they have asked questions about anything that is not clear and that they have understood the answers
- Knowing when each assignment is due

Ask the students to write down and tell the class something they do that helps them complete their homework successfully. Answers may include:

- Have the necessary supplies
- Make sure a time is set aside every day to study whether or not homework is assigned
- Get started
- In a planner, cross off completed assignments
- Keep all assignments in the same place *(Keep social studies work in a social studies folder, etc.)*
- Organize completed work and put it in one place so it is ready to pick up and take to school in the morning
- Make sure to turn homework in on time

There actually are students who do homework, but do not turn it in. Why do you think someone would do the work and then not turn it in? *(They might say the person: couldn't find the homework, forgot it at home, has a control issue and may be rebelling against a parent, etc.)* If someone mentions a student not handing in his/her homework as a way to rebel against a parent, point out that it is the student, not the parent, who suffers the consequences of this behavior.

What To Do If You Aren't In Class To Get An Assignment:

Ask the students what they do about homework when they are absent. Make sure their answers include:

- Designate a friend to get the assignment for them
- Call the homework hotline, if their school has one, to hear a recording of the assignments
- Look at the computer site, if their school has one, that lists homework assignments
- Have a parent call the teacher and ask if he/she may pick up the work
- Make sure to get the assignment when they return to school

Conclusion:

▸ Conclude the lesson by playing *Homework Bingo—Four In A Row*. Give each student a copy of the game. Ask the students to put a number in each circle, choosing from the numbers at the top of each column. The students are to choose numbers between and including those listed at the top of each column. Once everyone has finished, begin drawing numbers from the container. Students who have the number you call should raise their hands. Those who can answer the question in the space may cross off that space. The first person to cross off four spaces in a vertical, diagonal, or horizontal row or to cross off the four corners is the winner.

HOMEWORK BINGO—FOUR IN A ROW

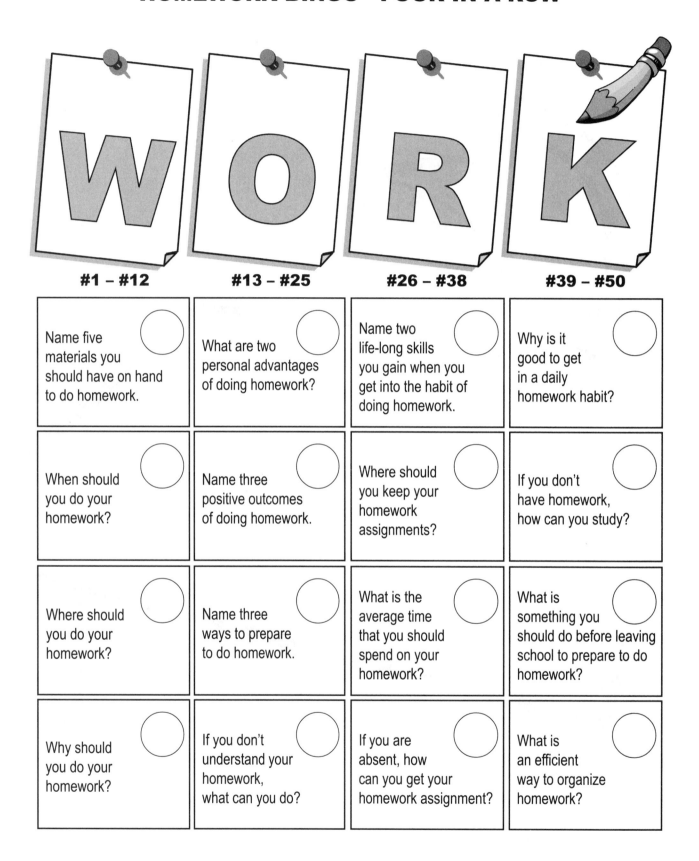

#1 – #12

#13 – #25

#26 – #38

#39 – #50

Name five materials you should have on hand to do homework.	What are two personal advantages of doing homework?	Name two life-long skills you gain when you get into the habit of doing homework.	Why is it good to get in a daily homework habit?
When should you do your homework?	Name three positive outcomes of doing homework.	Where should you keep your homework assignments?	If you don't have homework, how can you study?
Where should you do your homework?	Name three ways to prepare to do homework.	What is the average time that you should spend on your homework?	What is something you should do before leaving school to prepare to do homework?
Why should you do your homework?	If you don't understand your homework, what can you do?	If you are absent, how can you get your homework assignment?	What is an efficient way to organize homework?

HOMEWORK BINGO NUMBERS

1	2	3	4	5	6
7	8	9	10	11	12
13	14	15	16	17	18
19	20	21	22	23	24
25	26	27	28	29	30
31	32	33	34	35	36
37	38	39	40	41	42
43	44	45	46	47	48
49	50				

CLASSROOM GUIDANCE FROM A TO Z © 2007 MAR*CO PRODUCTS, INC. 1-800-448-2197

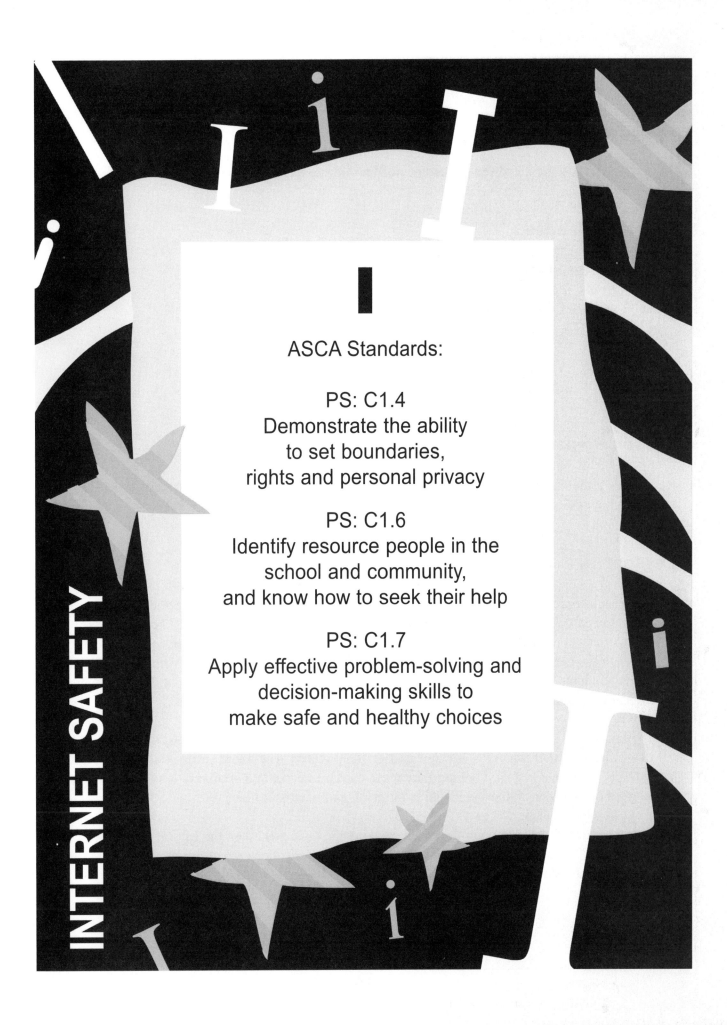

I

ASCA Standards:

PS: C1.4
Demonstrate the ability
to set boundaries,
rights and personal privacy

PS: C1.6
Identify resource people in the
school and community,
and know how to seek their help

PS: C1.7
Apply effective problem-solving and
decision-making skills to
make safe and healthy choices

INTERNET SAFETY

INTERNET SAFETY

Objective:

To help students understand the importance of learning to use the Internet safely

Materials Needed:

For each student:
- ☐ *Internet Safety Poster* (page 67) or *Internet Safety Bookmark* (page 68)
- ☐ 3 x 5 index card
- ☐ Pencil

For the leader:
- ☐ Scissors (optional)

Lesson Preparation:

Reproduce either the *Internet Safety Poster* or the *Internet Safety Bookmark* for each student. If you are using the bookmarks, cut them apart.

Lesson:

▸ Give each student a 3 x 5 index card. Ask each student to write three things about him/herself on the index card. Two of the statements should be true and one should be a lie. The students should not write their names on the index cards. Collect the cards. Redistribute them so that no one gets his/her own card. Ask the students to take turns reading aloud to the class what is on the index cards you have given them. Ask the student reading the card to guess which of the statements on the card is a lie.

▸ Explain that when a person doesn't know who wrote what he/she is reading, it is often hard to determine whether what was written is true. This is also true about information found on the Internet. People can post anything they want on the Internet and strangers who read their messages have no way of knowing what is the truth and what is a lie.

▸ Ask the students to give examples of lies that people have posted on the Internet. *(They may say that teens say they are older than they are, older people say they are younger than they are, some people lie about where they live or what their interests are, some males say they are females, and some females say they are males, etc.)*

▶ Discuss Internet safety.

Everyone needs to be concerned about Internet safety because anyone can write anything and you have no way of knowing if it is true. Teens are more likely to get into trouble than younger children and are more often preyed upon by sexual predators and child molesters. Millions of people go online every day and do not get into trouble or endanger themselves. They are safe because they know how to use the Internet wisely. Here are some safety tips based on the letters in the word *INTERNET*:

I Instant messaging—Be careful whom you instant message and what you say. Anything you write can be forwarded for anyone to read.

N Never give out personal information on the Internet without first checking with your parent/guardian. Don't add pictures, give phone numbers, etc. Once you give out personal information, you give up your privacy.

T Talk with your parents/guardians about their rules and expectations about your use of the Internet. Find out what sites you are allowed to visit and if there is a limit to how much time you may spend online. If you ever feel uncomfortable about something on the Internet, it is important to let your parents/guardians know.

E Enter chat rooms and social network sites cautiously. In most of these sites, everyone can see everything you write. Never write anything you would not say in public. Don't give out personal information that would let people figure out who you are and/or where you live or that might put you in danger. These sites can be the most dangerous areas on the Internet. If you visit them, be careful.

R Report to your parents/guardians if you are being harassed or threatened online. Report the problem to the cyber hotline.

N Never arrange to get together with someone you meet online. You really don't know if that person is who he/she claims to be. If someone you meet online wants to meet you in person, tell your parents/guardians.

E E-mail can be risky, too. Don't respond to spam mail or to people you don't know. Never send a photo or personal information to someone you don't know, even if that person says he/she knows you or your friends. Tell your parents/guardians if you get messages that are threatening, belligerent, or make you feel uncomfortable. Ask them to report the problem or report it yourself.

T Tell someone if you are being cyber-bullied. Talk with your parents/guardians if someone puts your secrets online, signs you up for contests, pretends to be you, posts your picture, gives out your personal information, and/or steals your password. If these things happen to you, change your password, change your e-mail address.

▶ Give each student an *Internet Safety* poster or a bookmark.

Conclusion:

▶ Conclude the lesson by saying:

The computer is an awesome tool. It is full of information. Use it in a safe way. Take time to be computer savvy!

INTERNET SAFETY POSTER

I
Instant message carefully.

N
Never give out personal information on the Internet without first checking with your parents/guardians.

T
Talk with your parents/guardians about their online rules for you.

E
Enter chat rooms and social networks cautiously.

R
Report if you are being harassed, threatened, and/or feel uncomfortable online.

N
Never arrange to get together with someone you met online.

E
E-mail has risks, too. Be aware of them.

T
Tell someone if you are being cyber-bullied.

Take time to be computer savvy and you will get the most benefits from the World Wide Web!

CLASSROOM GUIDANCE FROM A TO Z © 2007 MAR★CO PRODUCTS, INC. 1-800-448-2197

INTERNET SAFETY BOOKMARKS

INTERNET SAFETY!

I
Instant message carefully.

N
Never give out personal information on the Internet without first checking with your parents/guardians.

T
Talk with your parents/guardians about their online rules for you.

E
Enter chat rooms and social networks cautiously.

R
Report if you are being harassed, threatened, and/or feel uncomfortable online.

N
Never arrange to get together with someone you met online.

E
E-mail has risks, too. Be aware of them.

T
Tell someone if you are being cyber-bullied.

INTERNET SAFETY!

I
Instant message carefully.

N
Never give out personal information on the Internet without first checking with your parents/guardians.

T
Talk with your parents/guardians about their online rules for you.

E
Enter chat rooms and social networks cautiously.

R
Report if you are being harassed, threatened, and/or feel uncomfortable online.

N
Never arrange to get together with someone you met online.

E
E-mail has risks, too. Be aware of them.

T
Tell someone if you are being cyber-bullied.

INTERNET SAFETY!

I
Instant message carefully.

N
Never give out personal information on the Internet without first checking with your parents/guardians.

T
Talk with your parents/guardians about their online rules for you.

E
Enter chat rooms and social networks cautiously.

R
Report if you are being harassed, threatened, and/or feel uncomfortable online.

N
Never arrange to get together with someone you met online.

E
E-mail has risks, too. Be aware of them.

T
Tell someone if you are being cyber-bullied.

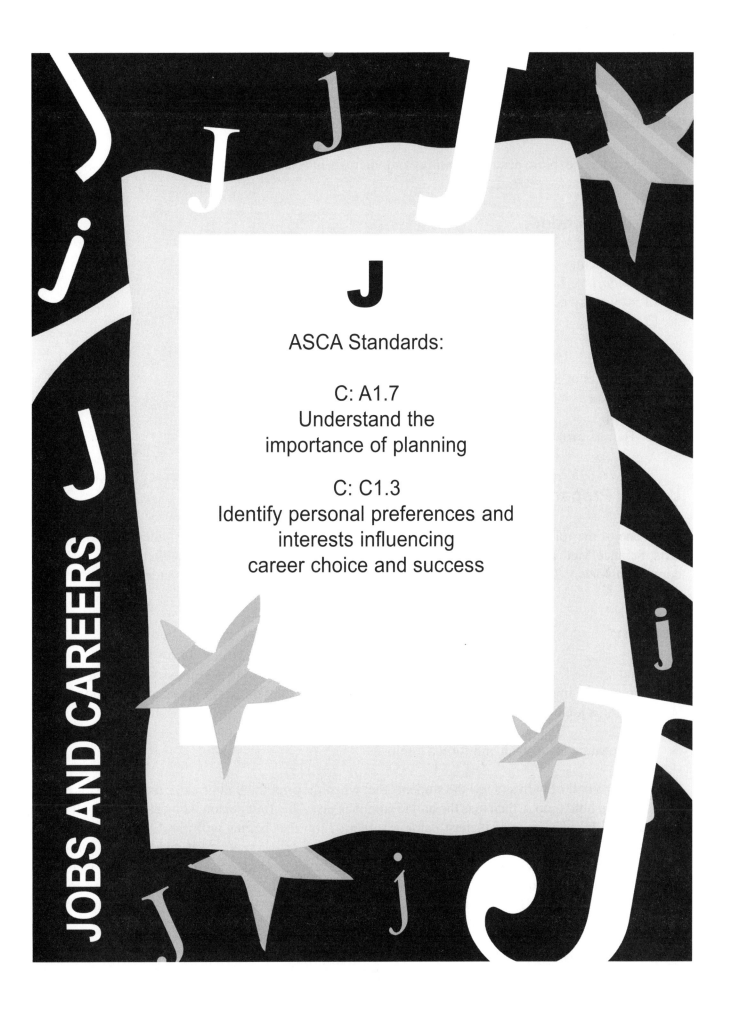

J

ASCA Standards:

C: A1.7
Understand the
importance of planning

C: C1.3
Identify personal preferences and
interests influencing
career choice and success

JOBS AND CAREERS

JOBS AND CAREERS

Objective:

To help students explore personal abilities and interests in relation to future careers

Materials Needed:

For each student:
- ☐ *Important To Me In My Job* (page 73)
- ☐ 4-5 sticky notes
- ☐ Pencil

For the leader:
- ☐ 7 pieces of 8 1/2" x 11" tagboard
- ☐ Marker
- ☐ Tape
- ☐ Ball of yarn

Lesson Preparation:

Write one of the following words or word pairs on each piece of tagboard: Computer/Technology, Arts, Science/Medicine, Social/Help People, Outside/Technical, Business, and Other. Reproduce a copy of *Important To Me In My Job* for each student. Gather the other needed materials.

Lesson:

▸ Introduce the lesson by telling the students that they are going to discuss jobs and careers, their interests, the importance of abilities and skills, and what they think is important to consider in choosing a job or career.

▸ Tell the students to stand and form a circle.

▸ Hold up a ball of yarn and tell the students that when they get the ball of yarn, they are to take a piece and hold onto it, then toss the ball to someone else. The first person who catches the ball of yarn and takes a piece of it must name a career or job that begins with the first letter of the alphabet. The next person to catch the ball of yarn and take a piece of it must name a job or career that begins with the second letter of the alphabet, and so on. For example, the leader catches the yarn, holds a piece of it, and says "A—architect." The leader tosses the yarn to a student, who says, "B—Bus Driver." That person holds a piece of yarn and tosses the yarn ball to another student, who will say "C" and so on, going through the alphabet from A to Z. If there are more than 26 students, the students will start again with A and continue until every student has had a chance to participate.

▸ Begin the activity.

▸ Tell the students to return to their seats. Give each student 4-5 sticky notes and assign each student one letter of the alphabet. Have the students write as many jobs or careers as they can think of that begin with their assigned letter, using one career for each sticky note. For example, the student with the letter *A* may write *architect, artist, astronaut,* or *art teacher.*

▸ As the students are completing the task, post the tagboard signs in various parts of the room.

▸ Explain to the students that technology may include jobs that involve working with computers or may require the skill to repair or build computers or other electronic equipment. The arts may include jobs like singing, dancing, acting, writing, or designing. Science and/or medicine includes jobs that require testing, experimenting, research, etc. Social service jobs are jobs in which people help, teach, or care for others. Jobs in business may include sales, hiring, managing, or working with data. Outside or technical jobs are jobs where people work outdoors; build; work with animals, nature, the environment; etc. Jobs that don't fit into any of these categories can be listed under *Other.* Emphasize that the students should try their best to fit each job into a posted category.

▸ Have the students post their sticky notes with jobs written on them under the category that best describes the kind of job each one is. Review each category and read the jobs the students have listed in that category. If there is some question about whether a job belongs in a particular category, discuss its placement with the students. Be sure to discuss how some jobs could be listed in more than one category.

▸ Give each student a copy of *Important To Me In My Job.* Ask the students to write, on the lines extending from the circle, some things that are important to them when thinking of a job or career. Have them tell the class what they value and what they want. If necessary, give the following examples of things they might choose:

   • Money
   • Travel/no travel
   • Co-workers
   • Dress
   • Work schedule
   • Option to work independently
   • Bonuses

Ask the students if anyone would like to share what he/she has written.

▶ Tell the students to consider their abilities when choosing a job or career. Ask for examples of how the lack of certain abilities prevents people from choosing certain jobs. Some answers might be:

- If you have a difficult time speaking to people, you probably don't want to be a salesperson.
- If you can't carry a tune, you won't want to be a singer.
- If you have difficulty writing, you probably won't want to be a newspaper reporter.
- If you can't stand the sight of blood, you probably don't want to be a nurse.

▶ Tell the students to think about the following suggestions when deciding on a job or career:

- It is important to focus on your abilities and what you are realistically able to do.
- When considering various careers, you should choose a few and try to have some experiences in those areas. If you want to be a veterinarian, for example, you could volunteer at an animal shelter.
- Job shadowing is an effective way to find out if you might like a job. You can spend a day with someone who does the kind of work in which you are interested.
- Determine how to reach your goal and take steps to get there. In high school, for example, make sure you schedule classes that will benefit you in your possible career choice. Ask your school counselor for help with planning what subjects to take in order to reach your goal.
- Explore where you can go after high school for training. If you will be going to college, learn how to look at colleges and see what different schools have to offer. If you are interested in a job that requires technical training, attend a vocational school that meets your needs while you are still in high school and/or after you graduate.

Conclusion:

▶ Conclude the lesson by emphasizing that the students should think about and plan for the career they choose. Encourage them to begin now. Let them know they may change their mind many times, and that this is OK. Tell them to look at the things that interest them in relation to their skills and abilities. Finally, tell them to find out what they have to do to reach their goal and take those steps.

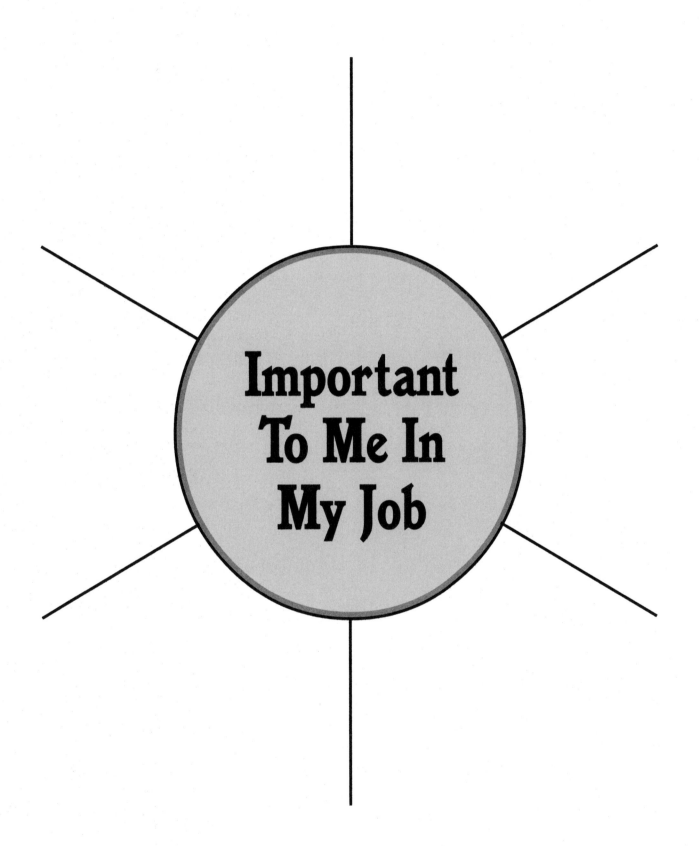

73

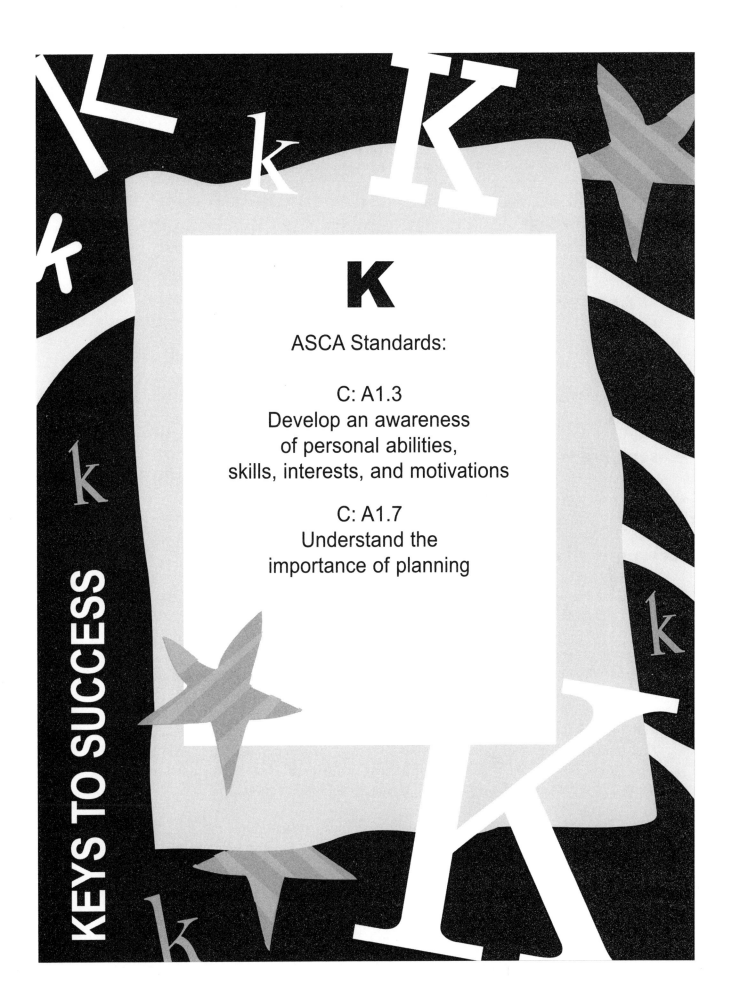

K

ASCA Standards:

C: A1.3
Develop an awareness
of personal abilities,
skills, interests, and motivations

C: A1.7
Understand the
importance of planning

KEYS TO SUCCESS

KEYS TO SUCCESS

Objective:

To help students learn what steps to take in order to successfully reach a goal

Materials Needed:

For each student:
- ☐ *Keys To Success* (pages 78-79)
- ☐ Piece of yarn
- ☐ Pencil
- ☐ Scissors

For the leader:
- ☐ Several hole punches

Lesson Preparation:

Reproduce *Keys To Success* for each student. Gather the other needed materials.

Lesson:

▶ Introduce the lesson by telling the students that the dictionary defines *success* as *the achievement of something desired or favorable.*

▶ Have the students name some idioms that mean success. One example would be *with flying colors. (Other answers that may be mentioned are: A feather in one's cap, the sky is the limit, go far, go places, he/she made it, made good, etc.)*

▶ Tell the students to think of someone who has achieved success. It may be a parent who was the first in his/her family to graduate from college; or even someone like Martin Luther King Jr., who pursued his dream of equality for African-Americans. Have each student tell the class the name of the person he/she chose and the reasons for his/her choice.

▶ Give each student a copy of *Keys To Success,* a piece of yarn, a pencil, and scissors. Have the students cut out each key and punch out the holes in it. *(Note: The yarn will be used at the end of the lesson to connect the keys.)*

▶ Say to the students:

Look at the first key. It is blank. On this key, write something at which you would like to succeed. You may write one of your goals.

▶ Then have the students look at each key and review each key's tips for success.

- *Sail toward success.* Make a goal. Strive to reach your goal. Realize that there will be stumbling blocks along the way. On the back of this key, write one thing you can do to reach your goal and one stumbling block you may encounter along the way. When everyone has finished, those who wish to do so may share what they have written.
- *Utilize your talents and strengths.* On the back of this key, list the talents and strengths that will help you succeed.
- *Capitalize on opportunities.* Look for ways to successfully reach your goals. Recognize these opportunities and make the most of each of them. On the back of this key, write an example of an opportunity that may come your way.
- *Challenge yourself.* When things get tough, don't give up. On the back of this key, write an encouraging message you can say to yourself when things get tough. Something like: "I can do this!"
- *Empower yourself.* Take charge of you! No matter how much someone else wants you to succeed, only you can make it happen. Don't depend on others to make you happy or help you succeed. On the back of this key, write another encouraging message you can say to yourself. Something like: "I am not going to let others tell me I can't do this."
- *Start today.* Make a plan for how you are going to achieve your goals. On the back of this key, write the first thing you are going to do in your quest for success.
- *Share your success.* Once you reach your goal, share your success with others. Then it will be time for you to review, renew, and rethink what you are going to do next.

▶ Have the students thread the yarn through the holes of the keys to make a key ring.

▶ Collect the scissors and hole punches.

Conclusion:

▶ Conclude the lesson by telling the student that they hold the *Keys To Success* in their own hands.

KEYS TO SUCCESS

Sail toward success.

Utilize your talents and strengths.

Capitalize on opportunities.

KEYS TO SUCCESS

Challenge yourself.

Empower yourself.

Start today.

Share your success.

L

ASCA Standards:

PS: A1.5
Identify and express feelings

PS: C1.11
Learn coping skills for
managing life events

LOSS AND GRIEF

LOSS AND GRIEF

Objective:

To help students understand the grieving process

Materials Needed:

For each student:
- ☐ *Feelings Of My Heart* (page 85)
- ☐ Paper
- ☐ Pencil
- ☐ Crayons or markers

For the leader:
- ☐ Chalkboard and chalk or whiteboard and marker
- ☐ Book *Tear Soup* (optional)

Lesson Preparation:

Reproduce *Feelings Of My Heart* for each student. Gather the other materials.

Lesson:

▸ Introduce the lesson by asking the students to name the most obvious loss a person can experience. *(death)*

▸ Explain that loss occurs whenever the absence of someone or something creates a void or sense of emptiness.

▸ Ask what other situations could be considered losses. *(The children may suggest: themselves or a friend moving away, parents' divorce, sickness that deprived someone of good health, death of a pet, separation from a parent due to military service, etc.)*

▸ Tell the students to take out a piece of paper and a pencil, then to list the losses they have experienced. Allow those who wish to talk about their losses to do so.

▸ Have the students name feelings that people associate with loss. As the feelings are named, write them on the board. Some possibilities are:

sadness	pain	anger	difference
weirdness	loneliness	aloneness	confusion
fear	fury	being down	exhaustion
worry	anxiety	tiredness	lack of support
frustration	listlessness	feeling low	feeling ignored
depression	envy	distraction	annoyance
need to talk	withdrawal	irritation	being overwhelmed
misery	tension	melancholy	

▸ Reinforce the fact that all the words written on the board describe normal, healthy feelings. Remind the students that there are no good or bad feelings and that all feelings are OK. There is no right or wrong way to feel.

▸ Give each student a copy of *Feelings Of My Heart* and crayons or markers. Tell the students to think of a loss they have experienced. Tell them to color the heart with colors representing some of the feelings they have had as a result of this loss. After they color the heart, they are to put the color and the feeling word that each color represents on the lines below the drawing. *(Note: Be observant, because this may be a difficult activity for some students.)*

▸ Allow those who wish to share their experiences with the class to do so.

▸ **Optional Activity:** Read the book *Tear Soup* by Pat Schwiebert and Chuck DeKlyen aloud to the students. Discuss the meaning of the book and have each student write his/her own recipe for tear soup.

▸ Review the following comments about loss. Tell the students these are very important points to remember. Discuss each point.

- It has been said that people who experience a loss go through certain stages. All of these stages are necessary and healthy. The first stage is shock or disbelief which expresses itself in denial that the loss has occurred. A person going through the second stage may be really sad, depressed and/or angry. The third stage is bargaining. The now grieving person makes a bargain to bring their loved one back. Since this does not work, the griever experiences a degree of depression. In time, the person accepts the loss and is able to move on.
- Everyone experiences grief in a different way. The grief process may last for months or even years.
- No one "gets over" a loss. A person moves through the stages of grief and is finally able to cope more successfully, but does not "get over" the loss.
- The grief process doesn't move in a straight line. On some days, a person who has experienced a loss may feel OK, then feel sad or mad for the next day or two. This happens throughout the grieving process.

- Have an outlet for your grief. Talk with someone about your loss. Draw, write, exercise, etc.
- Realize that there will be changes within your family. You may change, and the way you spend holidays or even ordinary days may be different. Friends may not act the same. Some of these changes you may like. You may dislike others.
- Take care of yourself. Know that there are people who will support you and listen to you. Reach out to those people.
- Grief is a process. Experience all your feelings. Focusing on happy memories of your loved one may help fill the emptiness you feel.

▸ Tell the students to turn over their *Feelings Of My Heart* activity sheet and write two or three memories of the person or situation they lost. Tell them to think of things that make them smile. Emphasize that focusing on happy memories will help get rid of the emptiness and/or pain they may feel. Allow those students who wish to do so to share their memories with the class.

▸ Collect the crayons or markers.

Conclusion:

▸ Conclude the lesson by encouraging the students to ask questions about loss and grief. Let the students know that if they need someone to talk with, you are available.

FEELINGS OF MY
HEART

_____

_____

_____

_____

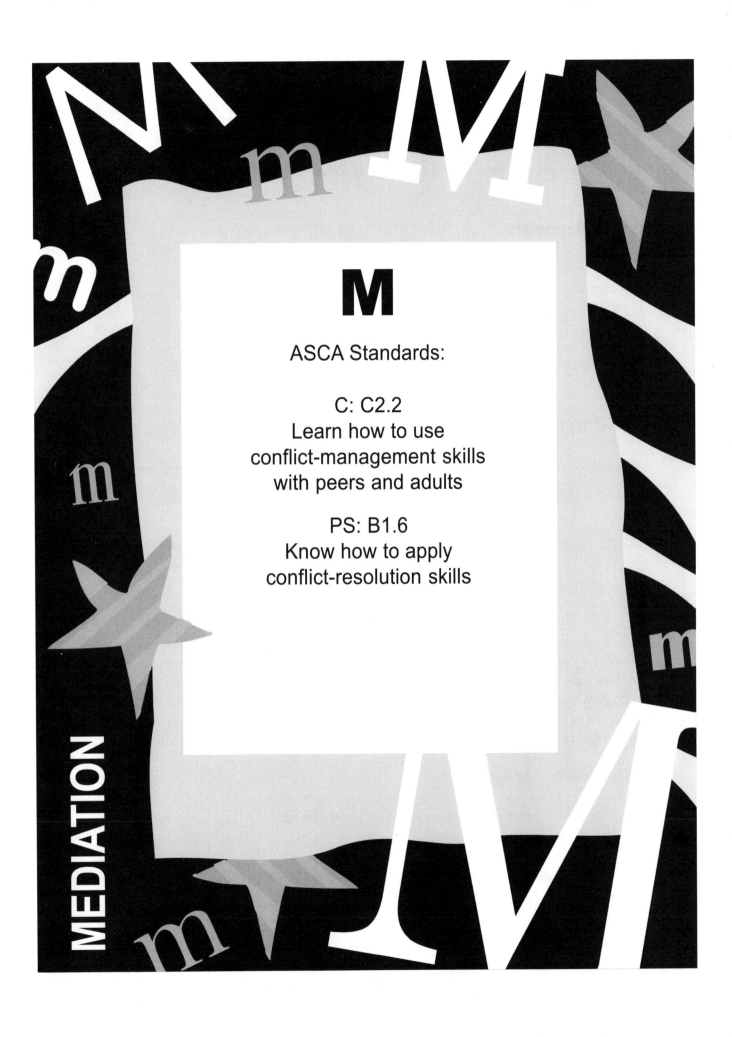

M

ASCA Standards:

C: C2.2
Learn how to use
conflict-management skills
with peers and adults

PS: B1.6
Know how to apply
conflict-resolution skills

MEDIATION

MEDIATION

Objective:

To help students learn and practice mediation techniques

Materials Needed:

For each student group:
- ☐ 3 *Mediation Contracts* (page 93)
- ☐ Pencil

For the leader:
- ☐ *Mediation Contract* (page 93)

Lesson Preparation:

Reproduce three copies of the *Mediation Contract* for each student group and one copy for the leader.

Lesson:

▸ Introduce the lesson by having the students tell the class what the word *mediation* means to them.

▸ Explain that mediation is a process by which an unbiased person helps others resolve their differences in a peaceful way. In school, mediations don't make students become friends. Mediation does help the student involved understand the other person and gives him/her an opportunity to present his/her side of an argument or dispute. In some cases, students agree to disagree. That is OK. The important thing is to resolve the conflict in a peaceful way. Tell the students that they are going to learn some mediation techniques and practice being mediators.

▸ Review the following steps:

1. Mediation takes place between two students at a time.

2. To participate in mediation, both students must agree that they want mediation to settle their argument or dispute. The students must also agree that they will follow the rules of mediation.

The rules of mediation are:

- Do not interrupt
- Stay seated
- Speak directly to the other person
- Work on the problem

3. Once the rules have been presented, the mediator will ask if the students agree to submit their argument or dispute to mediation and agree to follow the rules. Once the students agree, mediation can begin.

4. The mediator will ask which student wants to tell his/her side of the story first. That person must speak directly to the student with whom he/she is in conflict. Some examples of speaking directly are: "I heard you say …" or "I saw you do …" Do not say, "She said this" or "He did that." Speak directly to the other student, not to the mediator. Then let the other student tell his/her side of the story.

4. When each person finishes telling his/her side of the story, the mediator asks how he/she felt at the time of the conflict.

5. Each person will then repeat the other student's description of what happened and of how the other person said he/she felt at the time of the conflict.

6. The mediator will then take out a *Mediation Contract* to use for demonstration. The mediator will ask the first person what he/she needs from the second person. The mediator writes on the contract exactly what the first person says. The mediator repeats the process with the second person. When both students have expressed their needs, the mediator will read aloud what each student said and ask if the statements are correct or if either student wants to add anything else.

7. The mediator reads what the first person has said he/she wants and, after each request, asks the second person if he/she can honor the request. If the second person says he/she can honor the request, the mediator circles the request on the contract. After repeating the first person's requests and asking if the second person can grant each one, the mediator repeats the process with the second person's requests.

8. If the students cannot agree to honor each others' requests, the mediator should explain that sometimes a person cannot agree to do something another person wants. When this happens, the two people are said to agree to disagree. This is OK, but remember that it is never OK to hurt someone verbally, physically, or emotionally.

9. The mediator will again read what each person has agreed to do, making sure the students understand what has been said. If the students are in agreement with everything, the mediator will ask each student to sign his/her name at the bottom of the contract. The mediator will then sign his/her own name.

▸ Ask for two student volunteers to help with a demonstration of mediation. In this demonstration, the facilitator/counselor will be the mediator. Ask the students to come to the front of the room. Tell them you are going to help them mediate their problem of calling each other names. This is an example of the mediation procedure:

The mediator brings the students into the room and asks if they agree to submit their argument or dispute to mediation. If they do, the mediator will read the rules of mediation aloud (page 89) and ask if the students agree to follow them. If they agree to follow the rules, the mediation begins.

Ask who wants to tell his/her side of the story first. Remind the students to speak directly to the other person. A typical mediation may go like this:

Person A: I was in the hall, minding my own business, when you came up to me and started calling me names for no reason at all. I didn't do anything to you. In fact, I purposely stay away from you because I don't want problems.

Mediator: How did you feel when you were called names?

Person A: I felt mad. You'd feel mad, too.

Mediator: Person B, would you tell your side of the story? Person A, please listen without interrupting.

Person B: I heard from someone that you have been talking about me. You know that I hate it when people talk about me. That is why I called you names. No one is going to talk about me.

Mediator: How did it make you feel when you heard you were being talked about?

Person B: I was angry. No one is going to talk about me and get away with it.

Mediator: Person B, please rephrase what Person A has said about what happened and about how he/she feels.

Person B: Person A said he/she felt mad because I called him/her names in the hall.

Mediator: Person A, will you rephrase what Person B said?

Person A: Person B said he/she is mad because he/she heard I was talking about him/her, and he/she doesn't like people to do that.

Mediator: Is there any more discussion?

Person A: Yes, I want to tell Person B that I wasn't talking about him/her. All I said was, "Look at Person B. He/she is sitting with the new kid today." I didn't say anything else.

90

Person B: Thanks for telling me that. Someone said you called me a name because I was sitting with the new student.

Person A. I did not call you a name.

Mediator: Is there any more discussion? If not, let's write up a contract to help get this resolved. Person A, please tell me what you need from Person B.

As Person A speaks, the mediator writes what he/she wants, word for word, on the *Mediation Contract*:

> For Person B not to call me names.

> For Person B not to confront me in the hall.

> If Person B thinks I am doing something, he/she should ask me about it, not listen to and believe what others say about me.

Mediator: Anything else? *(Person A says there is not.)* Person B, what is it that you want from Person A?

As Person B speaks, the mediator writes what he/she says, word for word, on the *Mediation Contract*:

> For Person A not to talk about me.

> If Person A has something to say about me, he/she should say it to my face.

> That is all.

The mediator reads aloud what Person A wants and asks if he/she wants to add anything else. When Person A says he/she has nothing to add, the mediator does the same for Person B. Person B has nothing to add, either.

Mediator: Person B, will you agree to not call Person A names? *(If Person B agrees to this, the mediator circles this statement.)* Will you agree not to confront Person A in the hall? *(If Person B agrees, the mediator circles this.)* If you have a concern, will you ask Person A about it and not listen to or believe what the other kids say? *(If Person B agrees, the mediator circles this.)*

Mediator: Person A, do you agree to not talk about Person B? *(If Person A agrees, the mediator circles this statement.)* Do you agree to talk to Person B directly if you have something to say? *(If Person A agrees, the mediator circles this.)*

Mediator: Person A. You have agreed to not talk about Person B and to talk to him/her directly if you have something to say. Please sign here to indicate that you will do this. Person B, you have agreed to not call Person A names, not confront him/her in the hall, and to talk to him/her directly if you have something to say. To show that you agree, sign your name at the bottom of this contract.

Tell the students that a copy of the contract will be given to the school administrator. If the students break the contract, the school disciplinarian will decide what to do about it. Ask both students if anything else needs to be said. Thank the volunteers for their help and dismiss them to return to their seats.

▶ Have the students count off in groups of three. One person in each group will be *A,* another *B,* and the third *C.* One of the students in each group will be the mediator and the other two will be the students in conflict. The students should switch roles for each of the following three situations. The person chosen to be the mediator should use the *Mediation Contract* to practice the mediation process. Distribute three *Mediation Contracts* to each group, explaining that the contract should be used by the mediator in each situation. Make sure the students have pencils. Have the students select the mediator for the first situation. Then read the first situation.

Situation 1: Person A borrowed $2.00 from Person B more than a week ago and still has not repaid Person B. Person B wants his/her money now. Person C is the mediator.

After a reasonable amount of time, read the second and third situations. Allow time between reading each situation for the students to complete the task.

Situations 2 and 3: Person A called Person B and had Person C listen to the conversation on another phone line without Person B's knowledge. Person A purposely tricked Person B into saying something negative about Person C. Now Person B is mad at Person A, and Person C is mad at Person B. *(Note: This situation will require two mediations. The first mediation will be between Person A and Person B, and second one will be between Person B and Person C.)*

▶ Have some of the students share the results of their *Mediation Contracts* with the class.

Conclusion:

▶ Conclude the lesson by telling the students that mediation is an effective way to deal with conflict. The rules of mediation must be followed, and the students must remember that it is important for each person to be heard and for them to discuss the problem without attacking each other. It is also important for the students to talk about what each person needs and to come to a peaceful resolution of the argument or dispute.

MEDIATION CONTRACT

Mediations take place between two people with the help of a mediator. Before the mediation can begin, each person must agree to submit the argument or dispute to mediation.

Ask each person if he/she agrees to the following rules:

- ▶ Don't interrupt
- ▶ Stay seated
- ▶ Speak directly to the other person
- ▶ Work on the problem

Once each person agrees to follow the rules, the mediation may begin.

Have each student tell his/her side of the story, describing what happened and how it made him/her feel. Then have each student repeat what the other student said. Discuss what the students have said.

Have each student state what he/she needs from the other student. The mediator writes what each person says and circles, on the contract, what each student agrees to do. Everyone signs the contract.

	needs:		needs:

Student's signature _____

Student's signature _____

Mediator's signature _____

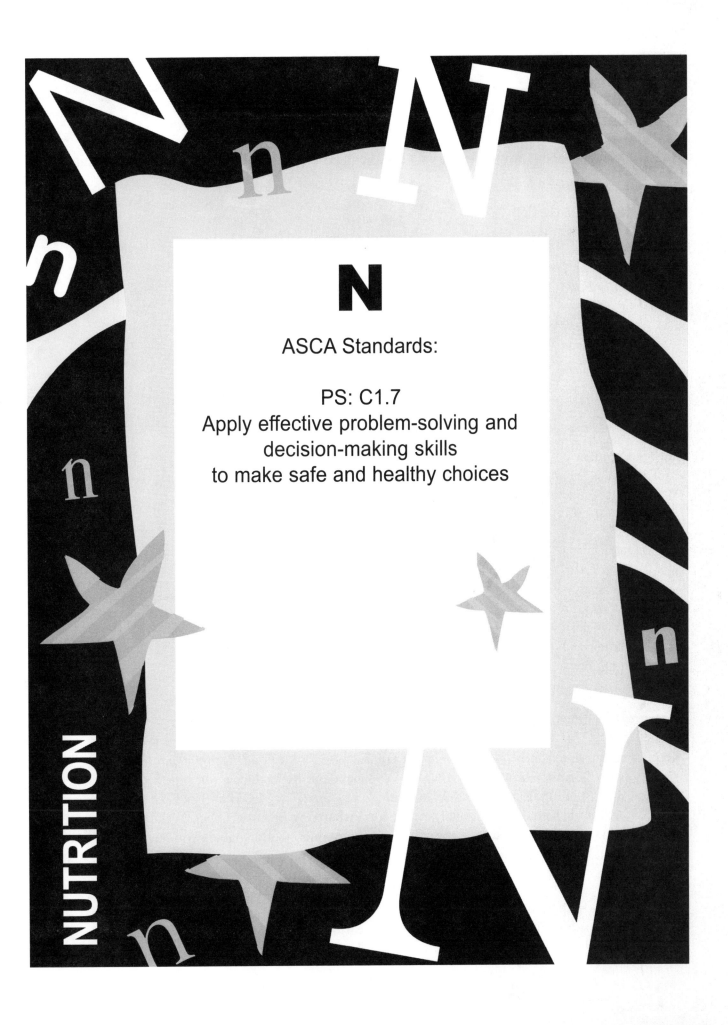

N

ASCA Standards:

PS: C1.7
Apply effective problem-solving and
decision-making skills
to make safe and healthy choices

NUTRITION

NUTRITION

Objective:

To teach students about proper nutrition and make them aware of their personal nutrition habits

Materials Needed:

For each student:
- ☐ *American Heart Association Guidelines: Daily Food Recommendations For Children Ages 9-13* (page 100)
  or
  American Heart Association Guidelines: Daily Food Recommendations For Adolescents Ages 14-18 (page 101)
- ☐ *Seven-Day Food Diary For Children Ages 9-13* (optional, page 104)
  or
  Seven-Day Food Diary For Adolescents Ages 14-18 (optional, page 104)
- ☐ Pencil

For each student group:
- ☐ *Package Label* (page 103)
- ☐ Package label
- ☐ Pencil

For the leader:
- ☐ *Food Label* (page 102)
- ☐ Transparency
- ☐ Overhead projector
- ☐ Craft sticks
- ☐ Marker
- ☐ Container

Lesson Preparation:

Reproduce the *American Heart Association Guidelines: Daily Food Recommendations For Children Ages 9-13* or *Adolescents Ages 14-18* for each student. Reproduce a *Package Label* worksheet for each student group. Reproduce a *Seven-Day Food Diary For Children Ages 9-13* or *Adolescents Ages 14-18* for each student (optional). Make a transparency of *Food Label*. Write each student's name on a craft stick and place the craft sticks in a container. Collect labels you have cut off packages from each of the six food groups. Make sure you have enough labels for each student group. For example:

Grain group—nutrition label from a loaf of bread
Milk group—nutrition label from a yogurt carton
Fat and Oil—nutrition label from a bottle of salad dressing

Meat and Bean—nutrition label from a package of chicken
Vegetable—nutrition label from a box of frozen vegetables
Fruit—nutrition label from a bag of grapefruit

Lesson:

▸ Introduce the lesson by telling the students that nutrition is very important to a person's health. Your goal is to raise students' awareness of the need for good nutrition. Tell the students you will review the new AHA daily food recommendations, talk about portion sizes, explain the importance of activity, and teach them how to read a food label.

▸ Distribute the appropriate copy of the *American Heart Association Guidelines: Daily Food Recommendations* to each student. Tell the students to follow along as each group is presented.

Grains:

The largest food group is *grains*. Ask the students for some examples of foods that are grains and write them on their worksheets. (*Bread, pasta, rice, cereal, crackers, oats, etc.*) Grains contain fiber, which makes us feel full.

Ask the students how many portions of grains they should eat each day. If the grain is not measured in ounces, one portion is one slice, $^1/_2$ cup, 1 cup cooked ready-to-eat cereal, or five crackers. By reading the package label, they can see what one portion (serving size) equals. At least half of these portions should be whole grains. Foods that contain whole grains are clearly labeled. Whole grains are not necessarily wheat, bran, or multi-grain. Ask if anyone can give examples of whole grains. (Brown rice, whole wheat, whole oats, wild rice, etc.) A person cannot tell by color if a product contains whole grains. A product must meet U.S. Food and Drug Administration guidelines to be labeled as containing whole grains. Whole grains contain dietary fiber that can help protect against diseases like heart disease and diabetes and also help control your child's weight.

Refined grains include white flour, white rice, and white bread. Fiber and vitamins are removed during the processing of refined foods, then added back in. Refined foods are not as healthful as whole-grain foods.

These foods are high in complex carbohydrates, which are the body's favorite fuel. They give you energy to play and pay attention in school. Ask the students to list, on the worksheet, some grains that they eat each day, then circle those foods listed that are whole grains Have the students share their answers with the class.

Vegetables:

Introduce the next group by asking the students to check their worksheets and see how many servings of vegetables they should eat every day. Vegetables are an excellent source of vitamins and minerals and are low in calories. Tell the students to look for dark-colored vegetables—greens and oranges—because these vegetables are especially rich in vitamins. It is best to eat fresh vegetables, because canned or frozen vegetables may be high in sodium. Ask the students to list, on the worksheet, some vegetables that they eat each day. Have the students share their answers with the class.

Fruit:

The next group is the *fruit* group. Ask the students to check their worksheets and see how many servings of fruit they should eat every day. Fresh fruit is best. Fruits are good sources of important vitamins like A and C. Tell the students they should drink only a limited amount of juice because juice has a high sugar content. Remind them to beware of the sugar in the syrup in canned fruit and to eat different fruits every day. Ask the students to write, on the worksheet, some examples of fruit they eat each day and to share their answers with the class.

Milk/Dairy:

Foods from this group help build strong bones and teeth. Tell the students they should eat three servings of food from this group every day. Servings of cheese and other foods from this group are measured in ounces. Remind the students to reduce fat intake by drinking low-fat milk or fat-free milk and eating low-fat yogurt. Cream cheese and butter are no longer a part of this food group. Ask the students to write, on the worksheet, some examples of milk or dairy products they eat each day and to share their answers with the class.

Lean Meat/Beans:

Ask the students to check their worksheets and see how many servings of lean meat or beans they should eat every day. The meat and bean group includes meat, poultry, fish, dry beans, eggs, and nuts. This food group provides protein. Protein helps your body maintain and repair body tissues and build muscle. Some healthy tips to remember are:

- Choose lean meats
- Don't cook or eat the skin on chicken
- Cut the fat off meat
- Don't bread meat, fish, or chicken
- Bake, grill, or broil meats, instead of frying them
- Include in your diet fish like salmon, trout, and herring, which are rich in omega 3 fatty acids

Ask the students to list, on the worksheet, examples of foods from this group that they eat each day and to share their answers with the class.

Fats, Oils, and Sweets:

Children and adolescents should limit fat and oils to five teaspoons per day. Oils are fats that are liquid at room temperature, like the vegetable oils, are commonly used in cooking. The most beneficial fats are monounsaturated and polyunsaturated fats. Students should avoid foods that are high in saturated and transaturated fats, like shortening and margarine. Ask the students to name some ways they get fat in their diets. *(They may name: cooking oils, nuts, fish, salad dressings, etc.)* It is also good idea to limit the amount of sugar you eat

98

because the body stores the extra sugar. That can lead to weight gain and other health problems. Tell the students to use fats and oils sparingly and to limit the amount of sweets they eat. Ask the students to write, on the worksheet, some examples of fats, oils, and sweets that they eat each day and to share their answers with the class.

▸ Review the following information with the students:

The American Heart Association (AHA) provides recommendations for a healthy diet. It is also important to balance food intake with physical activity. The amount of activity you perform and the amount of time it takes determine the number of calories you burn.

Ages 9-13: Boys should consume 1,800 calories a day. A boy who is physically active should consume between 2,000 and 2,200 calories per day. Girls should consume 1,600 calories a day. Girls who are physically active should consume between 1,800 and 2,000 calories a day.

Ages 14-19: Boys should consume 2,200 calories a day. A boy who is physically active should consume between 2,400 and 2,600 calories per day. Girls should consume 1,800 calories a day. Girls who are physically active should consume between 2,000 and 2,200 calories a day.

▸ Teach the students how to read food labels. On the overhead projector, display *Food Label*. As the students are looking at the food label, ask the following questions:

- How much is one serving? *(7 crackers)*
- How much fiber does this serving contain? *(3 grams)*
- How many calories does this serving contain? *(120 calories for 7 crackers)*
- How much fat does this serving contain? *(3 grams, calories from fat 25)*
- How much sodium does this serving contain? *(160 milligrams)*

▸ Tell the students that reading food labels will help them understand nutrition and follow the American Heart Association recommendations for a healthy diet.

▸ Divide the students into groups of four or five. To insure a random grouping, choose four or five craft sticks from the container. The students whose names are on the craft sticks will form the first group. Continue this process until every student is in a group. Give each group a package label and a copy of the *Package Label* worksheet. Have the students complete the worksheet together, then share their results with the class.

▸ **Optional Activity:** Give each student the appropriate copy of the *Seven-Day Food Diary*. Tell the students to keep track of what they eat, how many portions of various types of food they eat, and whether they are eating the correct number of servings from each food group. Have them do this for one week.

Conclusion:

▸ Conclude the lesson by reminding the students that making healthy and wise choices about what they eat is an important part of good health and that good health enriches a person's life.

AMERICAN HEART ASSOCIATION GUIDELINES:
DAILY FOOD RECOMMENDATIONS FOR CHILDREN AGES 9-13*

<u>CALORIES</u>

Girls: 1600 calories
Boys: 1800 calories

<u>FOOD GROUPS</u>	<u>RECOMMENDED AMOUNTS</u>	<u>ONE SERVING SIZE</u>
GRAINS	5-6 servings per day (Girls: 5 oz.—Boys: 6 oz.)	1 slice bread $^1/_2$ cup cooked pasta, rice, or cereal 1 cup cooked ready-to-eat cereal 5 crackers

Examples of grains I eat are:

Circle the foods that are whole grains.

VEGETABLES	4-5 servings per day (Girls: 2 cups—Boys: $2^1/_2$ cups)	$^1/_2$ cup cooked or chopped raw vegetables 1 cup raw, leafy vegetables $^3/_4$ cup vegetable juice

Examples of vegetables I eat or drink are:

FRUITS	3 servings per day (Girls and Boys: $1^1/_2$ cups)	1 medium apple, orange, banana, etc. $^1/_2$ cup canned, cooked, or chopped fruit $^3/_4$ cup juice

Examples of fruits I eat are:

MILK/DAIRY	3 servings per day (Girls and Boys: 3 cups)	1 cup milk or yogurt 2 oz. processed cheese $1^1/_2$ oz. natural cheese

Examples of milk and calcium I eat or drink are:

LEAN MEAT/BEANS	5 servings per day (Girls and Boys: 5 oz.)	1 oz. of meat, poultry, or fish $^1/_2$ cup cooked dry beans 1 egg 1 tablespoon peanut butter

Examples of meat and beans I eat are:

FATS, OILS, AND SWEETS	5 teaspoons per day (Girls and Boys: Fats and Oils: 25-35% calories)	

Examples of fats, oils, and sweets I eat or drink are:

*Taken from: http://www.americanheart.org

AMERICAN HEART ASSOCIATION GUIDELINES:
DAILY FOOD RECOMMENDATIONS FOR ADOLESCENTS AGES 14-18*

CALORIES

Girls: 1800 calories
Boys: 2200 calories

FOOD GROUPS	RECOMMENDED AMOUNTS	ONE SERVING SIZE
GRAINS	6-7 servings per day (Girls: 6 oz.—Boys: 7 oz.)	1 slice bread $1/2$ cup cooked pasta, rice, or cereal 1 cup cooked ready-to-eat cereal 5 crackers

Examples of grains I eat are:

Circle the foods that are whole grains.

VEGETABLES	5-6 servings per day (Girls: $2^1/2$ cups—Boys: 3 cups)	$1/2$ cup cooked or chopped raw vegetables 1 cup raw, leafy vegetables $3/4$ cup vegetable juice

Examples of vegetables I eat or drink are:

FRUITS	3-4 servings per day (Girls 1$1/2$ cups—Boys: 2 cups)	1 medium apple, orange, banana, etc. $1/2$ cup canned, cooked, or chopped fruit $3/4$ cup juice

Examples of fruits I eat are:

MILK/DAIRY	3 servings per day (Girls and Boys: 3 cups)	1 cup milk or yogurt 2 oz. processed cheese 1$1/2$ oz. natural cheese

Examples of milk and calcium I eat or drink are:

LEAN MEAT/BEANS	5-6 servings per day (Girls: 5 oz.—Boys: 6 oz.)	1 oz. of meat, poultry, or fish $1/2$ cup cooked dry beans 1 egg 1 tablespoon peanut butter

Examples of meat and beans I eat are:

FATS, OILS, AND SWEETS	5 teaspoons per day (Girls and Boys: Fats and Oils: 25-35% calories)	

Examples of fats, oils, and sweets I eat or drink are:

*Taken from: http://www.americanheart.org

FOOD LABEL

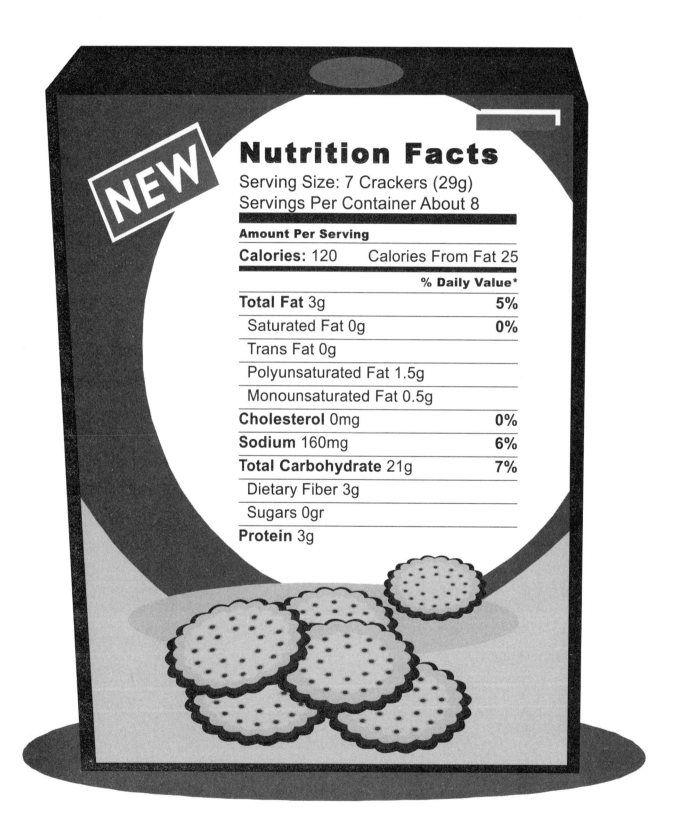

Nutrition Facts

Serving Size: 7 Crackers (29g)
Servings Per Container About 8

Amount Per Serving

Calories: 120 | Calories From Fat 25

	% Daily Value*
Total Fat 3g	5%
Saturated Fat 0g	0%
Trans Fat 0g	
Polyunsaturated Fat 1.5g	
Monounsaturated Fat 0.5g	
Cholesterol 0mg	0%
Sodium 160mg	6%
Total Carbohydrate 21g	7%
Dietary Fiber 3g	
Sugars 0gr	
Protein 3g	

NEW

PACKAGE LABEL

Product [   ]

How much is one serving? _____

How many servings are in the package? _____

How many calories are in one serving? _____

What is the total fat in one serving? _____

How much cholesterol is in one serving? _____

How much sodium is in one serving? _____

What are the total carbohydrates in one serving? _____

How much dietary fiber is in one serving? _____

How much sugar is in one serving? _____

103

SEVEN-DAY FOOD DIARY (AGES 9-13)	SEVEN-DAY FOOD DIARY (AGES 14-18)

SEVEN-DAY FOOD DIARY
(AGES 9-13)

MONDAY
Grains ☐☐☐☐☐☐ (Boys: 6, Girls: 5 servings)
Vegetables ☐☐☐☐☐ (Boys: 5, Girls: 4 servings)
Fruits ☐☐☐ (3 servings)
Lean Meat/Beans ☐☐☐☐☐ (5 servings)
Milk/Dairy ☐☐☐ (3 servings)
Fats/Oils ☐☐☐☐☐ (5 teaspoons)

TUESDAY
Grains ☐☐☐☐☐☐ (Boys: 6, Girls: 5 servings)
Vegetables ☐☐☐☐☐ (Boys: 5, Girls: 4 servings)
Fruits ☐☐☐ (3 servings)
Lean Meat/Beans ☐☐☐☐☐ (5 servings)
Milk/Dairy ☐☐☐ (3 servings)
Fats/Oils ☐☐☐☐☐ (5 teaspoons)

WEDNESDAY
Grains ☐☐☐☐☐☐ (Boys: 6, Girls: 5 servings)
Vegetables ☐☐☐☐☐ (Boys: 5, Girls: 4 servings)
Fruits ☐☐☐ (3 servings)
Lean Meat/Beans ☐☐☐☐☐ (5 servings)
Milk/Dairy ☐☐☐ (3 servings)
Fats/Oils ☐☐☐☐☐ (5 teaspoons)

THURSDAY
Grains ☐☐☐☐☐☐ (Boys: 6, Girls: 5 servings)
Vegetables ☐☐☐☐☐ (Boys: 5, Girls: 4 servings)
Fruits ☐☐☐ (3 servings)
Lean Meat/Beans ☐☐☐☐☐ (5 servings)
Milk/Dairy ☐☐☐ (3 servings)
Fats/Oils ☐☐☐☐☐ (5 teaspoons)

FRIDAY
Grains ☐☐☐☐☐☐ (Boys: 6, Girls: 5 servings)
Vegetables ☐☐☐☐☐ (Boys: 5, Girls: 4 servings)
Fruits ☐☐☐ (3 servings)
Lean Meat/Beans ☐☐☐☐☐ (5 servings)
Milk/Dairy ☐☐☐ (3 servings)
Fats/Oils ☐☐☐☐☐ (5 teaspoons)

SATURDAY
Grains ☐☐☐☐☐☐ (Boys: 6, Girls: 5 servings)
Vegetables ☐☐☐☐☐ (Boys: 5, Girls: 4 servings)
Fruits ☐☐☐ (3 servings)
Lean Meat/Beans ☐☐☐☐☐ (5 servings)
Milk/Dairy ☐☐☐ (3 servings)
Fats/Oils ☐☐☐☐☐ (5 teaspoons)

SUNDAY
Grains ☐☐☐☐☐☐ (Boys: 6, Girls: 5 servings)
Vegetables ☐☐☐☐☐ (Boys: 5, Girls: 4 servings)
Fruits ☐☐☐ (3 servings)
Lean Meat/Beans ☐☐☐☐☐ (5 servings)
Milk/Dairy ☐☐☐ (3 servings)
Fats/Oils ☐☐☐☐☐ (5 teaspoons)

SEVEN-DAY FOOD DIARY
(AGES 14-18)

MONDAY
Grains ☐☐☐☐☐☐☐ (Boys: 7, Girls: 6 servings)
Vegetables ☐☐☐☐☐☐ (Boys: 6, Girls: 5 servings)
Fruits ☐☐☐☐ (Boys: 4, Girls: 3 servings)
Lean Meat/Beans ☐☐☐☐☐☐ (Boys: 6, Girls: 5 servings)
Milk/Dairy ☐☐☐ (3 servings)
Fats/Oils ☐☐☐☐☐ (5 teaspoons)

TUESDAY
Grains ☐☐☐☐☐☐☐ (Boys: 7, Girls: 6 servings)
Vegetables ☐☐☐☐☐☐ (Boys: 6, Girls: 5 servings)
Fruits ☐☐☐☐ (Boys: 4, Girls: 3 servings)
Lean Meat/Beans ☐☐☐☐☐☐ (Boys: 6, Girls: 5 servings)
Milk/Dairy ☐☐☐ (3 servings)
Fats/Oils ☐☐☐☐☐ (5 teaspoons)

WEDNESDAY
Grains ☐☐☐☐☐☐☐ (Boys: 7, Girls: 6 servings)
Vegetables ☐☐☐☐☐☐ (Boys: 6, Girls: 5 servings)
Fruits ☐☐☐☐ (Boys: 4, Girls: 3 servings)
Lean Meat/Beans ☐☐☐☐☐☐ (Boys: 6, Girls: 5 servings)
Milk/Dairy ☐☐☐ (3 servings)
Fats/Oils ☐☐☐☐☐ (5 teaspoons)

THURSDAY
Grains ☐☐☐☐☐☐☐ (Boys: 7, Girls: 6 servings)
Vegetables ☐☐☐☐☐☐ (Boys: 6, Girls: 5 servings)
Fruits ☐☐☐☐ (Boys: 4, Girls: 3 servings)
Lean Meat/Beans ☐☐☐☐☐☐ (Boys: 6, Girls: 5 servings)
Milk/Dairy ☐☐☐ (3 servings)
Fats/Oils ☐☐☐☐☐ (5 teaspoons)

FRIDAY
Grains ☐☐☐☐☐☐☐ (Boys: 7, Girls: 6 servings)
Vegetables ☐☐☐☐☐☐ (Boys: 6, Girls: 5 servings)
Fruits ☐☐☐☐ (Boys: 4, Girls: 3 servings)
Lean Meat/Beans ☐☐☐☐☐☐ (Boys: 6, Girls: 5 servings)
Milk/Dairy ☐☐☐ (3 servings)
Fats/Oils ☐☐☐☐☐ (5 teaspoons)

SATURDAY
Grains ☐☐☐☐☐☐☐ (Boys: 7, Girls: 6 servings)
Vegetables ☐☐☐☐☐☐ (Boys: 6, Girls: 5 servings)
Fruits ☐☐☐☐ (Boys: 4, Girls: 3 servings)
Lean Meat/Beans ☐☐☐☐☐☐ (Boys: 6, Girls: 5 servings)
Milk/Dairy ☐☐☐ (3 servings)
Fats/Oils ☐☐☐☐☐ (5 teaspoons)

SUNDAY
Grains ☐☐☐☐☐☐☐ (Boys: 7, Girls: 6 servings)
Vegetables ☐☐☐☐☐☐ (Boys: 6, Girls: 5 servings)
Fruits ☐☐☐☐ (Boys: 4, Girls: 3 servings)
Lean Meat/Beans ☐☐☐☐☐☐ (Boys: 6, Girls: 5 servings)
Milk/Dairy ☐☐☐ (3 servings)
Fats/Oils ☐☐☐☐☐ (5 teaspoons)

O

ASCA Standards:

PS: C1.7
Apply effective problem-solving and
decision-making skills
to make safe and healthy choices

ODOR AND PROPER HYGIENE

ODOR AND PROPER HYGIENE

Objective:

To help students identify the elements of good hygiene as it pertains to adolescents

Materials Needed:

For each student group:
- ☐ *Hair, Face, Mouth, Body,* or *Hands & Feet* (pages 110-114)
- ☐ Pencil

For the leader:
- ☐ 5 different-colored chips or slips of paper
- ☐ Container

Lesson Preparation:

Have enough chips/slips of paper for each student in the class. Divide the colors equally and put them into the container. Reproduce one copy of *Hair, Face, Mouth, Body,* or *Hands & Feet* for each student group.

Lesson:

▶ Introduce the lesson by telling the students that they will be talking about a sensitive issue, *body odor*. They may wonder why it is necessary to talk about something like this, but the topic is important because the bodies of middle school students are going through many changes. One of these changes involves sweat glands, and the students may not realize these glands are becoming more active.

▶ Divide the students into five equal-sized groups. Do this by having each student take a colored chip/slip of paper from the container. The color chosen will indicate the group to which each student belongs.

▶ Assign a part of the body to each group. Tell the students they will be required to complete two exercises. The first exercise will be for each group to brainstorm how to ensure good hygiene for the part of the body assigned to it. The second part of the activity is to role-play a commercial, using a product that will help improve the hygiene of that body part. The commercial must state why the product is important to achieving the needed result for that part of the body.

106

▶ Assign a color and a number to each group. The groups are:

Group #1—Hair
Group #2—Face
Group #3—Mouth
Group #4—Body
Group #5—Hands and feet

▶ Distribute the appropriate worksheet to each group. Tell the students to list, on the worksheet, health habits necessary for the specific body part assigned to their group. When everyone has finished listing the health habits, the students are to think of a 30-second commercial for a product for this body part and role-play the commercial for the class. Remind them to focus on why the product is important for good hygiene. Tell the students they have 20 minutes to complete both activities.

▶ Begin with Group #1. Listen to and discuss what the group members say about good hygiene for hair. Remind the students to:

- Wash your hair on a regular basis—wash, rinse, wash again, then use conditioner if necessary. *(Teens' hair often is oily and must be washed often to be kept clean.)*
- Comb and brush your hair regularly.
- Have your hair cut and styled on a regular basis.
- There are a variety of hair products to help keep your hair healthy and looking nice. Can you name some of these products? *(They may name: gel, mousse, hairspray, dandruff shampoo, products specifically for oily hair, etc.)*

Have the students role-play their commercial.

▶ Have Group #2 discuss good hygiene for the face, excluding the teeth and mouth. Remind the students to:

- Wash your face at least when you get up every morning and every night before you go to bed.
- Use a gentler soap on your face than you use when you bathe or shower. Deodorant soap is harsh, so it is not good to use a deodorant soap on your face.
- Some adolescents get pimples. Heredity, stress, and/or hormones may trigger pimples. You can buy soaps, creams, and lotions to clear up pimples. If you have a lot of pimples or these products do not clear up the pimples you have, you should see a dermatologist, who can prescribe stronger medication to clear up your skin.
- Protect your face in the sun by using sunscreen.
- As boys get older, they will develop facial hair and start to shave. There are products available to protect your skin from irritation while you are shaving.
- Drink lots of water.

Have the students role-play their commercial.

▶ Have Group #3 share what the group members came up with on how to take care of the teeth and mouth. Remind the students to:

- Brush often, especially after eating breakfast and before going to bed.
- Floss regularly.
- Brush your tongue as well as your teeth.
- Get a dental checkup every six months.
- Watch your diet: The average can of pop/soda contains 10 teaspoons of sugar.
- If your lips are dry, use a lip gloss or moisturizer.
- If you have bad breath, even after brushing, try using mouthwash or breath mints.

Have the students role-play their commercial.

▶ Have Group #4 talk about good hygiene for the body. Remind the students to:

- Bathe or shower daily.
- Wash under your arms or use disposable wipes that contain soap if you can't bathe or shower for some reason.
- Use deodorant.
- Remember that powder can help absorb sweat.
- Wear clean clothes every day, because clothing absorbs sweat.
- Wear cotton or natural-fiber clothing and/or loose-fitting clothing if you sweat a lot.
- Girls who choose to shave their legs will have to do so on a regular basis.
- Protect exposed areas of your body from the sun by using sunscreen.

Have the students role-play their commercial.

▶ Have Group #5 discuss how to take care of the hands and feet. Remind the students to:

- Wash hands regularly, especially before eating, after using the restroom, and playing with pets.
- Use plenty of soap and water to wash your hands and take your time. Sing a song like *Happy Birthday* and don't finish lathering your hands until you finish singing.
- Keep your fingernails and toenails clean.
- Don't let your nails get too long, because long nails snag on clothing and other things.
- Use manicure scissors to cut away loose skin around your nails.
- Don't chew or bite your nails.
- Feet sweat, too.
- Wash your feet with soap every day.
- Change your socks every day.
- If foot odor is a problem, you can try some products that you can buy without a prescription. If these products don't eliminate your foot odor, your doctor can recommend something stronger.

Have the students role-play their commercial.

Conclusion:

▸ Conclude the lesson by telling the students that a healthy diet and healthy habits play a key role in good hygiene. To have good hygiene, they should:

- Avoid cigarette smoking, which causes wrinkles, yellows teeth and hands, promotes bad breath, makes clothing stink, and causes cancer and other diseases.
- Be careful of drinks like coffee, tea, and cola, which may contain caffeine and stain teeth.
- Limit the amount of sweets they eat.
- Eat a healthy diet.
- Get plenty of exercise.

Allow students who wish to do so to add other suggestions.

▸ Tell the students that since they will have their bodies for many, many years, they need to be conscious of what they do now to prevent health problems later in life. Remind them to be good to themselves and to practice good hygiene.

HAIR

FACE

MOUTH

BODY

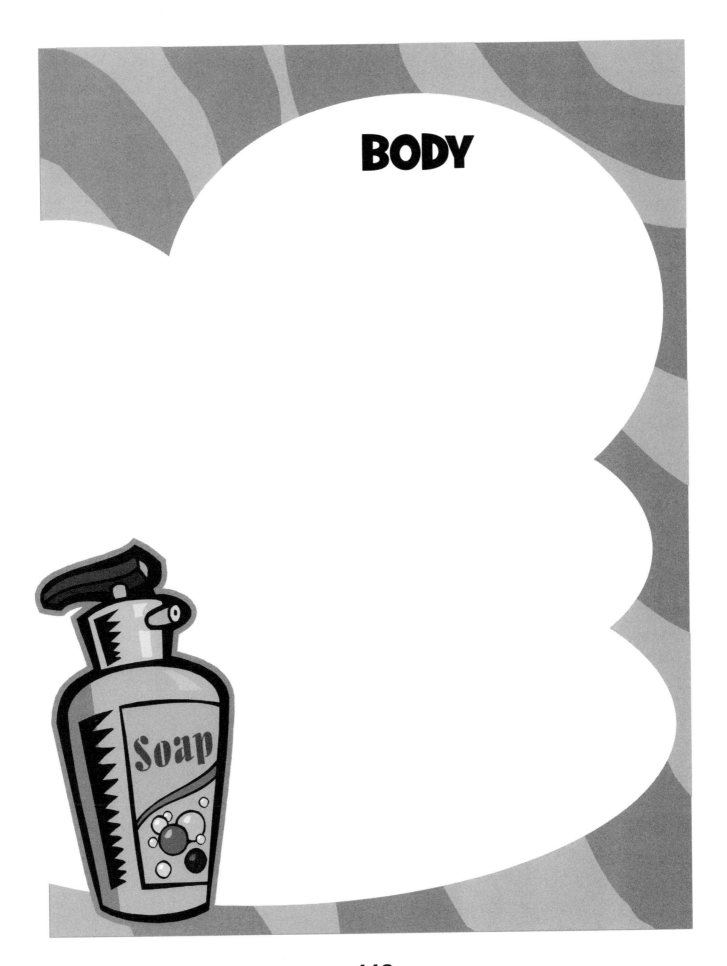

HANDS & FEET

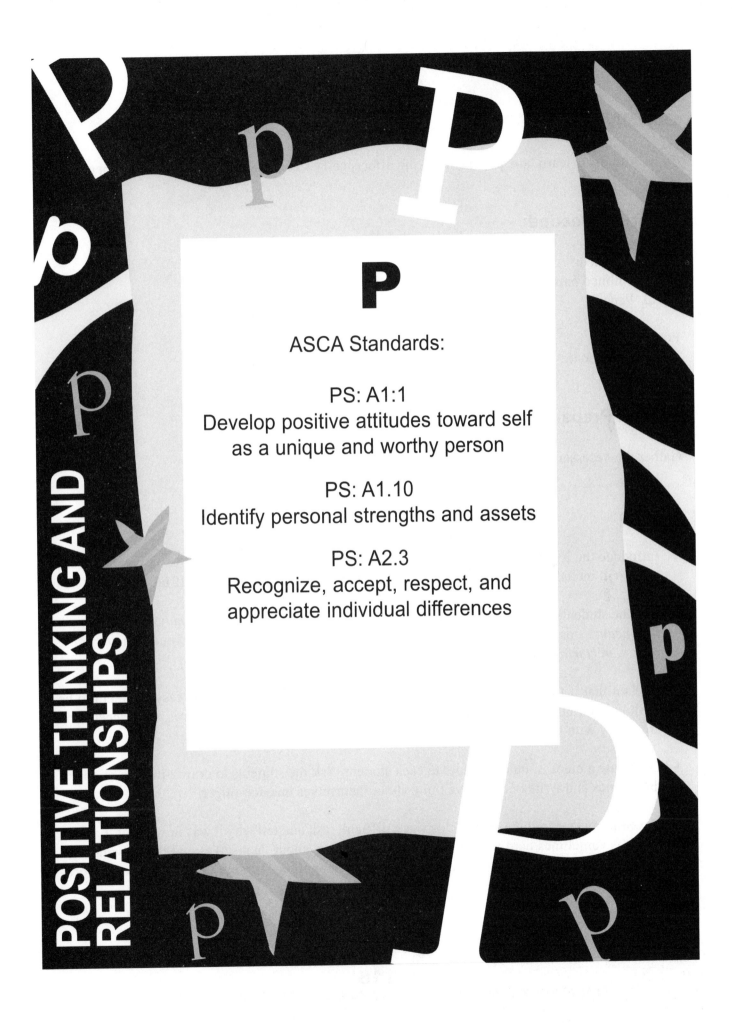

POSITIVE THINKING AND RELATIONSHIPS

P

ASCA Standards:

PS: A1:1
Develop positive attitudes toward self
as a unique and worthy person

PS: A1.10
Identify personal strengths and assets

PS: A2.3
Recognize, accept, respect, and
appreciate individual differences

POSITIVE THINKING AND RELATIONSHIPS

Objective:

To help students learn how positive thinking affects self-esteem and relationships with others

Materials Needed:

For each student:
- ☐ Unlined paper
- ☐ Pencil

For the leader:
- ☐ Chalkboard and chalk or whiteboard and marker

Lesson Preparation:

Gather the necessary materials.

Lesson:

▶ Introduce the lesson by telling the students that they will be talking about being positive. This topic will include positive social relationships and positive thinking and self-talk.

▶ Ask the students to tell the class what being positive means to them. *(They may say being positive means: treating themselves and others with respect, appreciating differences, encouraging others, nurturing, being responsible, etc.)*

▶ Explain that if the students have a positive attitude about themselves, it is easy for them to be positive with others. This is because when people are happy with themselves, they accept and are happy with others.

▶ Distribute a piece of unlined paper to each student. Ask the students to draw a picture of one of their hands and write one positive thing about themselves on each finger.

▶ Have the students tell the class if this was a difficult task and tell why it was or was not. Explain that it is sometimes hard for adolescents to be positive about themselves and that anyone who feels this way may have to work on feeling positive about him/herself. One way to begin working on this is for the students to give themselves positive messages.

CLASSROOM GUIDANCE FROM A TO Z © 2007 MAR*CO PRODUCTS, INC. 1-800-448-2197

▶ Give the students some examples of negative thoughts and ask for volunteers to turn them into positive thoughts. Suggest the following negative thoughts:

NEGATIVE THOUGHTS	POSSIBLE POSITIVE THOUGHTS
I can't do this.	I will try my best to do this.
I am so dumb. I did poorly on the test.	I will learn from my mistakes.
My hair looks crazy today.	Thank goodness, there's always tomorrow.
Sue won't be my friend.	That is her loss. I will still be nice to her.

Ask the students to give more examples of negative thoughts. Write their suggestions on the board and ask other students to turn them into positive thoughts.

▶ Tell the students that it is important not to let others pull them down. If someone says something negative to them, for example, they can let the remark bounce off and tell themselves what that person says doesn't matter. They can also say something positive to themselves to replace the negative statement/thoughts.

▶ Emphasize the importance of self-talk in creating positive self-esteem.

▶ Talk about interacting with others in a positive way.

▶ Have the students take out a piece of paper and a pencil with an eraser. Ask them to write down something negative that they may have said or heard. When everyone has finished, have the students wad up or wrinkle the paper, then smooth the paper out and erase what they wrote. What will happen? *(The paper will never be as smooth as it was before and it will be impossible to completely erase what was written.)*

▶ Ask the students what they think the purpose of this activity is. *(The answer is that saying negative or hurtful things leaves a mark that doesn't go away, even if the person tries to retract them. This is one reason why it is very important to think before you speak.)*

▶ Ask the students to recall the conversation in the movie *Bambi* between *Thumper* and his mother. *(She said, "If you can't say something nice about someone, don't say anything at all.")* This is a good motto to live by. Negative comments hurt and stay with people. Be positive not only with yourself, but also to others.

▶ Have the students take out another piece of paper and write their names across the top of the paper. When you say, "Pass," they are to pass their paper to the person behind them. The student in the last seat of each row should give his/her paper to the student in the front seat of the row to his/her left. The student in the last seat of the last row should give his/her paper to the student in the front seat of the first row. Each person is to write something positive on the paper about the person whose name is written at the top of the paper. Remind the students that when writing the positive comments, they should write something sincere and personal. Some examples could be to write about something they like about the person, something they appreciate about him/her, thank him/her for something, or describe something the other person did that the person writing the comment noticed and/or appreciated.

117

▶ Continue this activity until all the papers have been passed around the classroom and everyone has written something positive about each person. *(Note: As the students are doing this activity, walk around the room and read what they are writing. This will deter students from writing negative comments about their classmates.)*

▶ When everyone has his/her original paper, allow time for the students to read what their classmates have written about them. Encourage them to keep the paper in a safe place and, whenever they are feeling low or sad, pull out the paper and read it.

Conclusion:

▶ Conclude the lesson by reinforcing the fact that people who are positive with others will feel good about themselves and raise their own self-esteem.

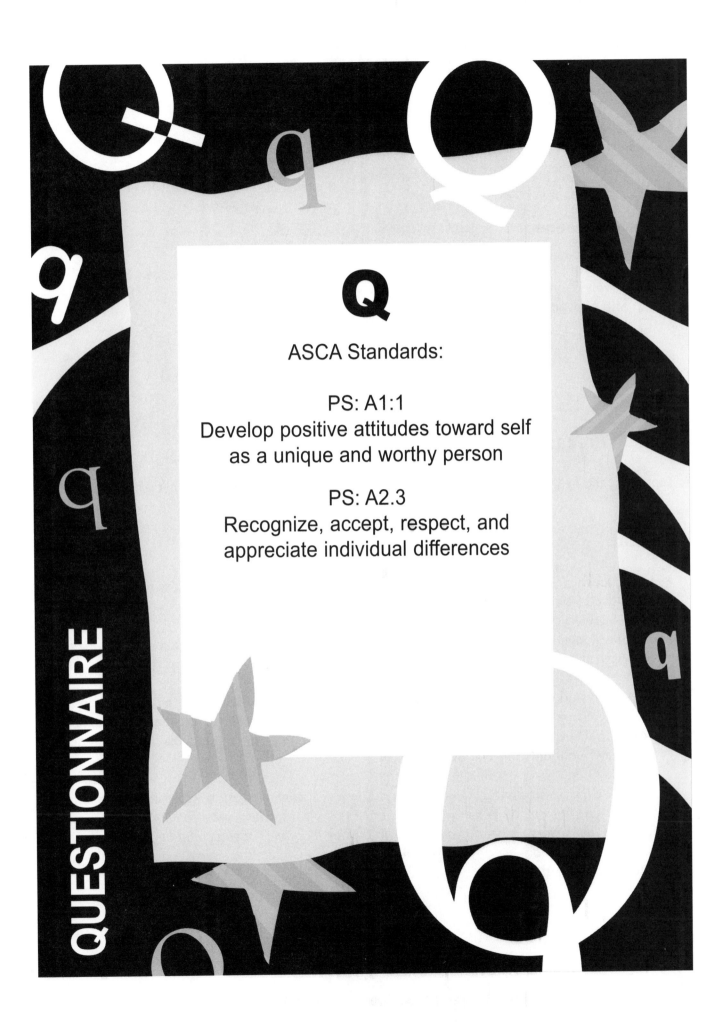

Q

ASCA Standards:

PS: A1:1
Develop positive attitudes toward self
as a unique and worthy person

PS: A2.3
Recognize, accept, respect, and
appreciate individual differences

QUESTIONNAIRE

QUESTIONNAIRE

Objective:

To help students become more aware of others

Materials Needed:

For each student:
- ☐ *People Search Questionnaire* (page 122)
- ☐ Slip of paper
- ☐ Pencil

For the leader:
- ☐ Container

Lesson Preparation:

Reproduce the *People Search Questionnaire* for each student. Gather the other necessary materials.

Lesson:

▶ Introduce the lesson by telling the students that they will spend the entire class period getting to know each other.

▶ Tell the students that it is important to get to know others, and that when they do, they may be surprised at what they learn.

▶ Give each student a copy of the *People Search Questionnaire* and a slip of paper. Explain that the students are to walk around the room and find students who can answer the questions in the boxes on their papers. Each student who answers a question initials the box. Tell the students they may initial only one box on each paper.

▶ Introduce the next activity, *Everyone Has A Story*. Ask each student to write, on his/her slip of paper, a question that could be asked of anyone in the class. *(Where were you born? Do you have brothers and sisters? What do you like to do in your free time? If you could be principal of this school, what would you do? What is your dream? etc.)* Collect the slips of paper and put them into the container.

▸ Ask each student to come to the front of the class and draw five slips of paper from the container. The questions should then be read, one at a time, and answered. When the first student has answered all five questions, he/she should tell the class one more thing about him/herself. The slips of paper are then put back into the container and another student continues the activity until everyone in the class has had a turn to answer five questions.

Conclusion:

▸ Conclude the lesson by asking the students to take a minute to think about how many new things they learned about their classmates during this activity. Go around the room and have each student tell something they learned about one person in the class.

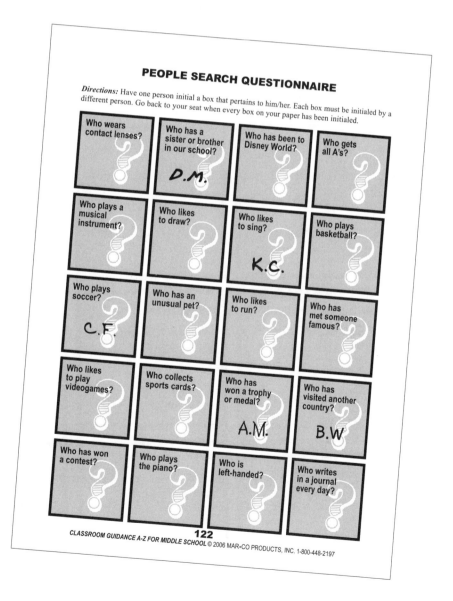

PEOPLE SEARCH QUESTIONNAIRE

Directions: Have one person initial a box that pertains to him/her. Each box must be initialed by a different person. Go back to your seat when every box on your paper has been initialed.

Who wears contact lenses?

Who has a sister or brother in our school?

Who has been to Disney World?

Who gets all A's and B's?

Who plays a musical instrument?

Who likes to draw?

Who likes to sing?

Who plays basketball?

Who plays soccer?

Who has an unusual pet?

Who likes to run?

Who has met someone famous?

Who likes to play videogames?

Who collects sports cards?

Who has won a trophy or medal?

Who has visited another country?

Who has won a contest?

Who plays the piano?

Who is left-handed?

Who writes in a journal every day?

RELATIONAL AGGRESSION

R

ASCA Standards:

PS: A2.3
Recognize, accept, respect, and appreciate individual differences

PS: A2.7
Know that communication involves speaking, listening, and non-verbal behavior

PS: A2.8
Learn how to make and keep friends

PS: C1.6
Identify resource people in the school and community, and know how to seek their help

RELATIONAL AGGRESSION

Objective:

To help students understand the components of relational aggression and learn strategies for dealing with it

Materials Needed:

For each student:
- ☐ Map of the school or sticky notes
- ☐ Pencil

For the leader:
- ☐ Masking tape
- ☐ Chalkboard and chalk or whiteboard and marker (optional)

Lesson Preparation:

Using the masking tape, make a line on the floor long enough for every student to stand on. Obtain a map of the school or sticky notes for each student.

Lesson:

▶ Introduce the lesson by telling the students that they will be talking about relational aggression, which is often associated with "mean girls."

▶ Have the students form a straight line on the masking tape, standing shoulder to shoulder and holding hands with the person standing next to them.

▶ Tell the students you are going to ask them a series of questions. If they answer "yes" to a question, they are to cross the line, but still hold onto the hands of the classmates standing on their left and right. The students are to go back to their original position every time you ask a new question. *(Another option would be to have the students who answer "yes" to a question move to designated areas in the room.)*

▶ Ask the following questions:

- Has anyone ever rolled his or her eyes at you?
- Have you ever rolled your eyes at someone?
- Has anyone ever ignored you?

- Have you ever ignored anyone?
- Have you ever been the subject of a rumor?
- Have you ever repeated a rumor?
- Has anyone ever been nice to you to your face then talked about you behind your back?
- Have you ever been excluded?
- Have you ever excluded someone else?
- Has anyone ever gossiped about you?
- Have you ever gossiped about anyone?
- Has anyone ever called you and tried to get you to say something negative about a person you didn't know was listening to the conversation?
- Have you ever called someone on the telephone and tricked him or her into saying negative things about a third person, who was secretly listening to your conversation?
- Have you ever been cyber-bullied?
- Have you ever cyber-bullied anyone?

▸ Have the students return to their seats.

▸ Ask how the students felt about this activity; what they think of gossip, rumors, rolling eyes, etc.; and how those behaviors make them feel.

▸ Tell the students this kind of behavior is called *relational aggression*. It happens every day in schools and the purpose of this lesson is to make the students aware of this behavior, let them know what to do if it is happening to them, and have them stop behaving this way if they are doing so. Relational aggression is behavior that is intended to hurt another person.

▸ Tell the students to be aware of the following types of situations involving relational aggression:

- Someone directs you to behave in a way that would hurt another person, but will not take any responsibility for telling you what to do
- Someone you thought you could trust uses against you information that you gave him/her
- Someone is nice to your face, but gossips about you behind your back
- Someone bumps, shoves, or in some other way picks on weaker people
- Someone wants you to change
- Someone makes you choose between friends

▸ Ask the students what they can do if they are a victim or a witness to these kinds of behaviors. *(They may say they can make an excuse and leave the situation, use an "I" message such as: "I feel betrayed when someone proves I can't trust him or her," walk away, report the behavior to an adult, etc.)*

▸ Tell the students that if someone is being hurtful to them, they must report it. There is a difference between tattling and telling. Tattling is reporting something just to get someone into trouble. Telling is reporting something in order to put a stop to dangerous or hurtful behavior. Telling is part of being assertive, and being assertive is standing up for yourself or others and saying that you are not going to allow hurtful behaviors to go on.

▸ Now that everyone knows what relational aggression is, ask the students where this kind of behavior takes place. Distribute a map of the school to each student. Have the students mark in pencil the areas on the map where relational aggression takes place. Have the students share and make note of others' answers about the areas where this happens most often. *(Note: If school maps are not available, distribute several sticky notes to the students and have them write on them the names of places in the school where relational aggression takes place. Post the notes on the board.)*

Conclusion:

▸ Conclude the lesson by emphasizing the importance of treating people with respect. Remind the students that if they cannot say anything nice to or about someone, they should not say anything at all.

▸ **Optional Activity:** You may end the lesson by asking the students if they would like to participate in a school-wide activity to reinforce the importance of accepting others and treating everyone with respect. Ask for their ideas. One idea you may suggest is a *Positive Attitude Week*. Teachers will be given slips of paper before the start of this week. If they see someone being positive to others, helping them out, performing random acts of kindness, etc., they give a slip of paper to that student. The student writes his/her name on the paper and puts it into a box in the school office. Names are drawn daily for such prizes as pizza coupons, fast food coupons, lunch with a favorite teacher, etc.

S

ASCA Standards:

PS: C1.10
Learn techniques for managing
stress and conflict

STRESS

STRESS

Objective:

To help students identify stressful situations and learn stress-management strategies

Materials Needed:

For each student:
- ☐ Paper
- ☐ Pencil
- ☐ 2 plastic cups, 2 tablespoons, school glue, craft stick (For Optional Activity #1)
- ☐ Paper plate, bubble wand, bubble solution (For Optional Activity #2)

For the leader:
- ☐ Beach ball or playground ball
- ☐ Masking tape
- ☐ Marker
- ☐ Borax detergent, food coloring, warm water (For Optional Activity #1)

Lesson Preparation:

Write each of the following situations on a piece of masking tape and tape it to the ball:

Going to high school
Didn't make the team
Got a job
Parents' divorce
Sibling goes away to college
Good grades
Volunteer work
Babysitting
Have a clean room
Got a new pet
Best friend moved away
Walk to school
Research paper due
Have detention after school

Gather any other needed materials.

Lesson:

▸ Introduce the lesson by telling the students that they will be talking about how to manage stress.

▸ Have the students take out paper and pencil and list the 10 most stressful things in their lives. *(They may list things like: school, tests, other kids, siblings, parents, homework, sports, schedule, teachers, lunchroom, P.E. class, etc.)* Discuss what they have included in their lists.

▸ Tell the students that stress isn't always a bad thing. Sometimes stress motivates people to do well. Ask the students to give some examples of stress that is good. *(Studying for a test and then doing well on the test, completing and getting paperwork in for college, practicing for a big game, public speaking, etc.)* The important thing is how a person manages stress. It is important not to let stress take charge of your life.

▸ Begin with an imagery activity. Ask the students to close their eyes (or put their heads down on their desks) and get comfortable in their seats. Tell them:

> Imagine that you are about to go up an escalator. This escalator will take you to one of three places. You must choose where you want to go. The choices are stay in this room, visit with a friend, or go to your favorite place. Step on the escalator and get off at the place where you want to be.

▸ Give the students a couple of minutes, with their eyes closed/head on desk, to remain in the place they chose. At the end of the time, ask them to go back down the escalator. Then have them open their eyes/raise their heads.

▸ Have the students tell the class where they went and what they did. Reinforce the idea that this is a simple and quick way to relax when they feel stressed.

▸ Have the students describe other ways that they manage stress. If the following ideas are not suggested, mention them:

  - Deep breathing—practice inhaling slowly, then exhaling slowly a few times
  - Physical activity such as walking, playing basketball, soccer, etc.
  - Writing or journaling
  - Sharing stress by talking with someone
  - Exercise
  - Music, listening or playing
  - Positive self-talk
  - Managing time more effectively

▸ Tell the students that looking for the positive in things is also a way to relieve stress. Focusing on the negative uses a lot of energy and will bring a person down. To help manage stress, always try to look at the positives. There is a saying that *behind every cloud, the sun is shining.* Look for that sun.

▸ Throw the ball to a student. Tell the student who catches the ball to look at the paper strip nearest his/her left thumb and read the strip aloud. Then ask him/her to tell why the situation the strip describes could be stressful and to name one positive thing about the situation. If the strip said "detention after school," for example, the positive thing could be a chance to get homework done or to get any needed help with homework. After the student responds, he/she should throw the ball back to the leader, who continues to throw the ball until everyone has caught it.

▸ **Optional Activity #1:** Make flubber. Give each student two plastic cups, two tablespoons, a craft stick, and school glue. In one of the cups, have the students mix two tablespoons of warm water with two tablespoons of school glue. This cup will hold the food coloring if you decide to color the flubber. In the other cup, have the students mix $1/4$ cup of warm water with $3/4$ teaspoon of Borax. Stir the mixture until the Borax has dissolved. Then add two tablespoons of the Borax mixture to the glue mixture. Using the craft stick, rapidly mix the two solutions. Watch what happens! Enjoy playing with the flubber. *(Note: Be sure to ask if anyone is allergic to anything you are asking them to handle. You may want to provide food service gloves to the students.)*

▸ **Optional Activity #2:** Assign students to groups of four or five. Give each group a bubble wand and a paper plate covered with bubble solution. Ask the students to think of something stressful to them, dip the wand into the bubble solution, then blow their stress away.

Conclusion:

▸ Conclude the lesson by reminding the students that when they are feeling stressed, they should think of some of the things discussed during this lesson.

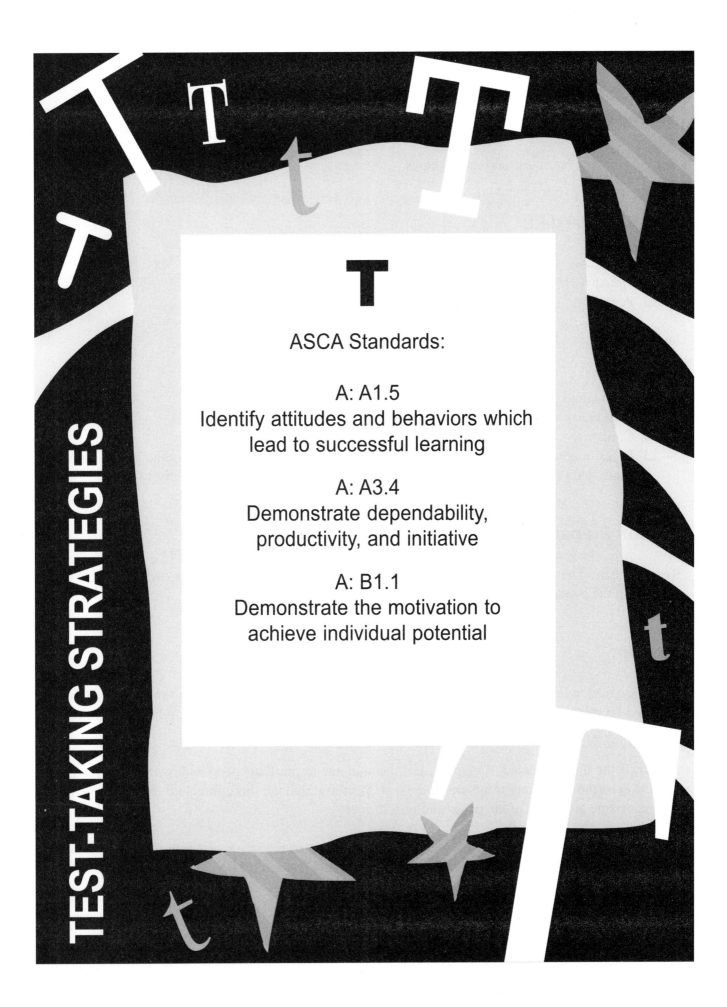

TEST-TAKING STRATEGIES

T

ASCA Standards:

A: A1.5
Identify attitudes and behaviors which lead to successful learning

A: A3.4
Demonstrate dependability, productivity, and initiative

A: B1.1
Demonstrate the motivation to achieve individual potential

TEST-TAKING STRATEGIES

Objective:

To help students learn test-taking strategies

Materials Needed:

For each student:
- ☐ *Timed Test* (page 135)
- ☐ Pencil

For the leader:
- ☐ Clock
- ☐ Chalkboard and chalk or whiteboard and marker
- ☐ Craft sticks
- ☐ Marker
- ☐ Container
- ☐ Paper, marker, tape, small plastic bags, pencils, breath mints, Smartie® candies, M-Azing® candy bars (To make the students' *Test Survival Kits* for the Optional Activity)

Lesson Preparation:

Reproduce the *Timed Test* for each student. Write each student's name on a craft stick and place the sticks into the container. Gather the other needed materials.

Lesson:

▸ Give each student a copy of *Timed Test*. Tell the students that this is a simple timed test that they have 10 minutes to complete. Tell them they should read the directions carefully before they begin.

▸ When the allotted time has elapsed, tell the students to put their pencils down. Then ask who followed the directions at the top of the test. Point out that the directions told them to just sign their name at the top of the paper and turn it over.

▸ Emphasize that when taking a test, it is very important to read directions carefully and follow them. This lesson will give the students other valuable test-taking tips.

▶ Begin by talking about preparing for a test. Ask the students to name some ways they prepare for a test. Write what they say on the board, making sure they include the following:

- Study—Avoid cramming. Review notes, make up and answer sample questions, memorize lists, look at the end-of-chapter reviews, review past tests and quizzes, have a parent quiz you.
- Get a good night's sleep (no *all-nighters*).
- Eat a good breakfast.
- Avoid arguments with family members, peers, etc.
- Make sure you have the necessary supplies (pencils, pens, erasers, calculator, etc.).
- Be on time. In fact, try to arrive a little early for the class.
- Have a positive attitude.
- Relax. Practice deep breathing, use positive self-talk.

▶ Ask the students for test-taking tips. Write their answers on the board, making sure to include the following:

- Read the directions first and make sure you follow them.
- Look over the test before you begin, so you have an idea what it is like.
- Answer all of the questions you know first, then go back and do the rest.
- Answer the questions with the greatest point value first.
- Don't spend too much time on any one question.
- Write clearly.
- Try not to leave any blanks.
- If you have extra time, check over your answers before turning the test in to the teacher.

▶ Ask the students what to do after they have completed a test. Write their answers on the board, making sure to include the following:

- Go back over the test and make sure you haven't left any blanks.
- If you have time, check over your answers.
- Don't worry if others finish the test before you do.
- Make sure your name is on the test paper.
- Turn your test in and relax. Tell yourself that you did the best you could.

▶ Review the following tips for specific types of questions.

- Essay—Be sure to read the directions carefully. Stick to the topic. Answer what is asked. Outline your answer to organize your thoughts. Watch the time to be sure you have enough time to answer every question on the test. Write legibly.

- Multiple-Choice Questions—Try to answer the question in your mind before looking at the choices on the test paper. If you can't answer the question, eliminate the choices you know are incorrect, then take an educated guess. Once you mark your answer, try not to go back and change. Unless you are absolutely sure your second answer is correct, your first guess is usually correct.

- True/False Questions—Do not leave any of these blank. Even if you do not know an answer, you have a 50-50 chance of getting it correct. Do not spend too much time on any one question. If part of a question or statement is false, the answer is false. Watch for statements that include words like *always, never, none, all,* because they are usually false. Statements that include words like *sometimes, most, usually, often,* and/or *many* are usually true. Sometimes one word will determine whether a statement is true or false.

Conclusion:

▶ Conclude the lesson with the following activity. By choosing craft sticks from the container, assign the students to groups of four. Once the students have been assigned to groups, ask each group to create a *Recipe For Taking A Test.* When every group has finished, have the groups share their recipes with the class. *(Note: You may want to copy the best recipes to share with other classes and/or grades. Post the recipes on the classroom bulletin board.)*

▶ **Optional Activity:** Give each student a *Test Survival Kit.* Do this by writing each of the following statements on a piece of paper and attaching the paper to the following items in parentheses. Then put everything in a small plastic bag. Give the bags to the students the day before a test.

- Take a deep breath, it will be OK. (breath mint)
- Stick to the point. (pencil)
- You are a smartie. (Smartie® candies)
- You are amazing. (M-Azing® candy bar)

TIMED TEST

Name _____

Directions: Read all of the questions and statements on this worksheet before you begin.

1. What is the capital city of your state? _____

2. Who is the president of the United States? _____

3. Whom would you like to meet? _____

4. What month were you born? _____

5. What is your middle name? _____

6. Who is our principal? _____

7. Finish this song, "Twinkle, twinkle, little _____."

8. What is your favorite subject? _____

9. What would you change about our school? _____

10. Do not answer questions 1-9. Sign your name at the top of the paper, then turn it over. Put your pencil down and wait for everyone else to finish. Please sit quietly.

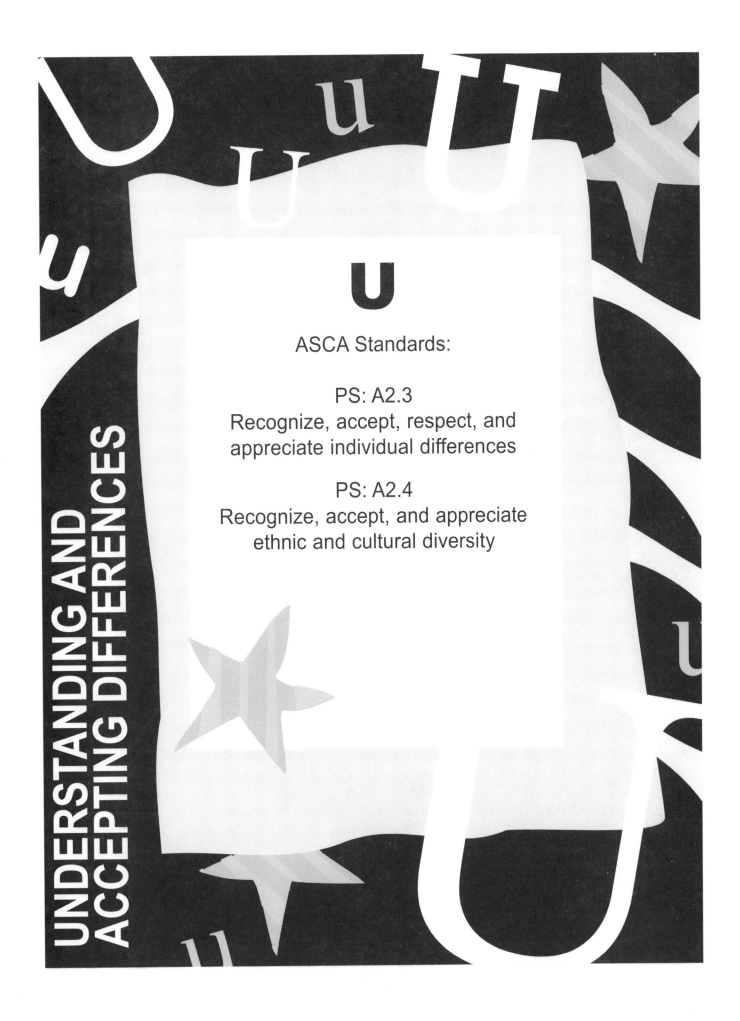

U

ASCA Standards:

PS: A2.3
Recognize, accept, respect, and appreciate individual differences

PS: A2.4
Recognize, accept, and appreciate ethnic and cultural diversity

UNDERSTANDING AND ACCEPTING DIFFERENCES

UNDERSTANDING AND ACCEPTING DIFFERENCES

Objective:

To help students understand the meaning and feelings of *prejudice* and behaviors that will eliminate prejudice

Materials Needed:

For each student:
- ☐ *Acceptance Bookmark* (page 149)

For the leader:
- ☐ Yellow sticky dots (enough for most of the class)
- ☐ 6 blue sticky dots
- ☐ 1 red sticky dot
- ☐ 1 green sticky dot
- ☐ *Word Cards* (pages 140-143)
- ☐ *Definition Cards* (pages 144-147)
- ☐ *Word And Definition Cards Answer Key* (page 148)
- ☐ Scissors
- ☐ Chalkboard and chalk or whiteboard and marker

Lesson Preparation:

Reproduce an *Acceptance Bookmark* for each student. Reproduce the *Word Cards* and *Definition Cards,* cut them apart, and divide them into two piles. Put the *Word Cards* in one pile and the *Definition Cards* in the other pile. Gather the other needed materials.

Lesson:

▸ Place a colored sticky dot on each student's forehead, but do not let the students know what color the dot is. Give most of the students a yellow dot. Give five or six students blue dots, and give one student a red dot and one student a green dot. *(Note: Be sensitive to which students receive the red and green dots. Choose students with high self-esteem.)*

- Tell the students that during this activity, they may only shake their heads "yes" or "no." They must find students with the same-colored sticky dot as they have and form groups according to the color of the dot, and they must do this without talking. A student may stand next to another student, look at a third student, then have the third student shake his/her head to indicate whether the first two students belong in the same group. The students will figure out their dot's color because other students will either exclude or include them in their group.

- When everyone has joined a group, there should be four groups: the large yellow group, the smaller blue group, one student in the red group, and one student in the green group. While the students are still in their groups, ask:

  - What does it feel like to belong to a group?
  - What does it feel like to be excluded from a group?
  - Ask the students with the red and green dots what it felt like when others would not let them join their groups.
  - What are some groups to which you belong?

- Tell the students that people have a basic need to belong. Our society sometimes puts people into groups based on a lot of different reasons and circumstances. What are some ways that people are divided into groups? *(People are grouped according to their race, age, gender, ability, socio-economic circumstances, etc.)*

- Explain that people judge others on the basis of the group to which they belong, rather than accepting them because they are unique. The purpose of this lesson is to make all of us aware of how people classify others into groups and the harm that can cause.

- Talk about words that are used when referring to *differences.* Distribute *Word Cards* to half of the students and *Definition Cards* to the other half. Have the students walk around the room to find a word and definition that match, then form a pair. Once students have formed a pair, they should stand with their partner until everyone else has done the same thing. Then they should hold their *Word* and *Definition Cards* so everyone in the class can see them. *(Note: An answer key for the Word and Definition Cards is found on page 148.)*

- Discuss the words and their definitions with the class.

- Ask the students what they can do to combat prejudice. Write their suggestions on the board.

Conclusion:

- Conclude the lesson by giving each student a bookmark.

- **Optional Activity:** Plan a service/learning project for the class. This may involve writing to the elderly, visiting a nursing home, visiting a preschool, or something else the students agree they would like to do. Service/learning projects are good opportunities for students to focus on such traits such as responsibility, empathy, and accepting others.

Exclusion

Aggression

Bias

Bigot

Homophobia

Prejudice

Racism

Stereotype

Injustice

Ignorance

Indifference

Sexism

Empathy

Inclusion

Peace

Agesim

Shutting out from consideration, privilege, membership—refusal to accept someone or groups of people

Unprovoked offense—forceful words or actions used to dominate others

Preconceived opinion about someone or something—holding a prejudice against someone or something

Someone who is narrow-minded, strongly intolerant of any belief, race, religion that is not his/her own

Fear of a person who has romantic desires for a person of the same sex

Unfavorable opinion or feeling formed in advance and without knowledge; preconceived judgment

Prejudice against people of a different origin

"Fixed image" of an individual or group

Unfairness; violation of another's rights

Lacking knowledge or information

Not caring, apathetic

Prejudice against people of a different sex, usually women

Identifying with another's situation, thoughts, feelings

Accepting others into a group, activity, relationship

A time when people feel safe and calm— get along with one another

Discrimination against someone of a certain age —especially older people

WORD AND DEFINITION CARDS ANSWER KEY

Agesim — Discrimination against someone of a ceratin age—especially older people

Aggression — Unprovoked offense—forceful words or actions used to dominate others

Bias — Preconceived opinion about someone or something—holding a prejudice against someone or something

Bigot — Someone who is narrow-minded, strongly intolerant of any belief, race, religion that is not his/her own

Empathy — Identifying with another's situation, thoughts, feelings

Exclusion — Shutting out from consideration, privilege, membership—refusal to accept someone or groups of people

Homophobia — Fear of a person who has romantic desires for a person of the same sex

Ignorance — Lacking knowledge or information

Inclusion — Accepting others into a group, activity, relationship

Indifference — Not caring, apathetic

Injustice — Unfairness; violation of another's rights

Peace — A time when people feel safe and calm—get along with one another

Prejudice — Unfavorable opinion or feeling formed in advance and without knowledge; preconceived judgment

Racism — Prejudice against people of a different origin

Sexism — Prejudice against people of a different sex, usually women

Stereotype — "Fixed image" of an individual or group

ACCEPTANCE BOOKMARKS

A Acknowledge that we are all unique.

C Care about others.

C Combat prejudice.

E Everyone deserves respect.

P Peace will come if we all get along.

T Take time to appreciate differences.

A Acknowledge that we are all unique.

C Care about others.

C Combat prejudice.

E Everyone deserves respect.

P Peace will come if we all get along.

T Take time to appreciate differences.

A Acknowledge that we are all unique.

C Care about others.

C Combat prejudice.

E Everyone deserves respect.

P Peace will come if we all get along.

T Take time to appreciate differences.

CLASSROOM GUIDANCE FROM A TO Z © 2007 MAR✷CO PRODUCTS, INC. 1-800-448-2197

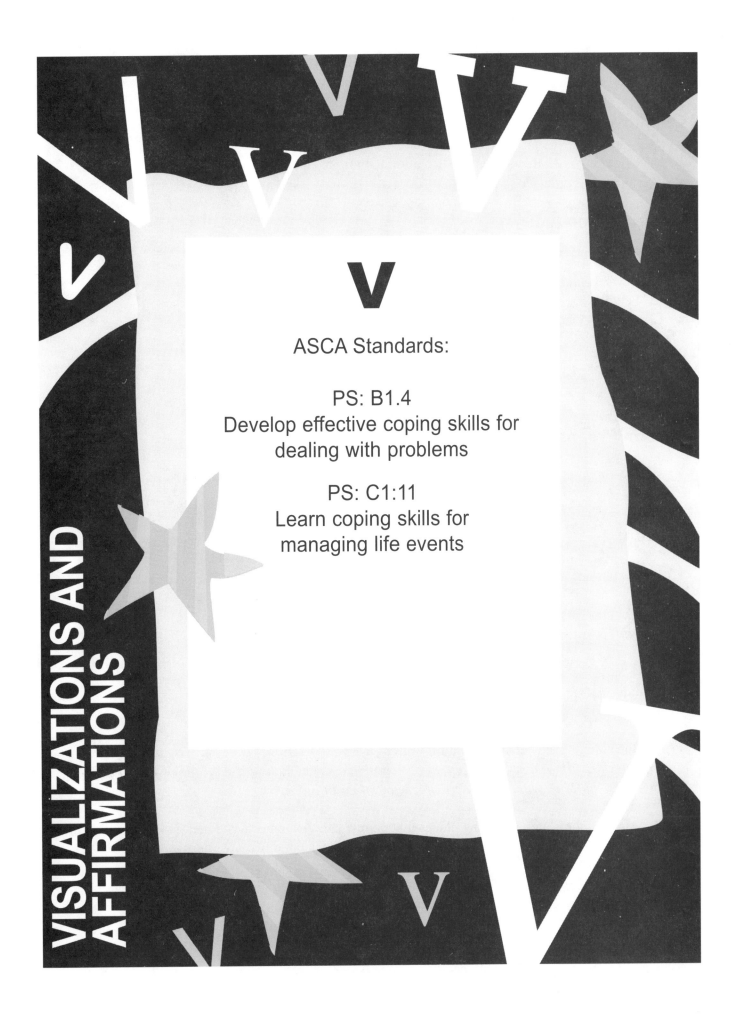

V

ASCA Standards:

PS: B1.4
Develop effective coping skills for
dealing with problems

PS: C1:11
Learn coping skills for
managing life events

VISUALIZATIONS AND
AFFIRMATIONS

VISUALIZATIONS AND AFFIRMATIONS

Objective:

To teach students visualization and affirmation techniques

Materials Needed:

For each student:
- ☐ *I Can Visualize* (page 155)
- ☐ Pencil
- ☐ 4-5 sticky notes

For the leader:
- ☐ Chalkboard and chalk or whiteboard and marker

Lesson Preparation:

Reproduce *I Can Visualize* for each student. Gather the other needed materials.

Lesson:

▸ Tell the students that this lesson begins with visualization and later includes affirmations.

▸ Ask the students the meaning of *visualization*. *(They may say visualization is when you: picture something in your head, talk to yourself and get into a peaceful state of mind, a quiet physical state, etc.)*

▸ Explain that people cannot run away from things, but we can create a sense of calmness and peace through visualization.

▸ Ask the students why someone would want to use visualization. *(They may say people use visualization to: calm themselves, get rid of negative energy, picture a goal they want to achieve, focus on what they want and where they want to go in life, etc.)*

▸ Have the students name calming places that people can visualize. Write their suggestions on the board. *(Examples are: ocean, desert, mountains, lake or pond, woods, their room, etc.)*

▸ Then have the students name calming things people can visualize. Write their suggestions on the board. *(Examples are: hammock, warm and soft blanket, rocking chair, swing, fire in a fireplace, pet, music, painting, favorite sport, talking with a friend or grandparent, etc.)*

▶ Have the students practice quiet imagery and visualization. Ask them to sit up straight and begin breathing slowly and evenly. Then ask them to close their eyes or to put their heads down on their desks. Tell them to visualize that they are at the ocean. Make the following statements aloud, pausing after each one:

- Hear the pounding of the waves.
- Watch the waves turn into ripples as they reach the shore.
- Listen to the birds.
- Feel the warm ocean breeze as it hits your face.
- Feel the sand beneath your feet.
- Listen.
- Feel.
- Watch.
- Listen.
- Feel.
- Watch.
- Just sit, listen to the sounds, see the sights, and feel nature.

▶ Ask the students to say *good-bye* to the scene, then open their eyes/lift their heads. Begin to discuss the activity by asking:

- How do you feel?
- What was it like?
- Was this hard to do?
- Where else could you visualize being?

▶ Distribute *I Can Visualize* to each student. Ask the students to write the name of or draw, in the bubble, something they can visualize. Allow those who wish to do so to share their ideas with the class. Practice visualizing two or three of the students' suggestions.

▶ Continue the discussion by saying that people can also use visualization to motivate themselves, get focused, get rid of negative energy, and/or get through a tough situation. Give the following examples:

- Winning at a sport
- A person who has a hard time speaking in public may want to visualize him/herself speaking in front of a crowd
- Getting along with someone you don't get along with
- Picture yourself doing well on a test
- Picture a goal you want to achieve
- Picture yourself being assertive
- Visualize accomplishing a difficult task

▶ Ask the students if they can think of other helpful visualizations people can use.

▸ Continue by saying that visualization can be a powerful tool to help us relax and/or achieve a goal.

▸ Explain that using affirmations is another powerful tool. Affirmations are positive self-talk a person can believe. Some examples of affirmations are:

- I can do this.
- I can learn from my mistakes.
- It is OK to ask for help.
- I am a good person.
- I am the best that I can be.

▸ Distribute four or five sticky notes to each student and have the students write an affirmation on each one. When the students have finished, ask them to stick their notes on the board. Read each affirmation aloud, then discuss it.

Conclusion:

▸ Conclude the lesson by telling the students that visualization and affirmations are two coping skills they can use to better themselves, set goals, help themselves relax, and build self-confidence.

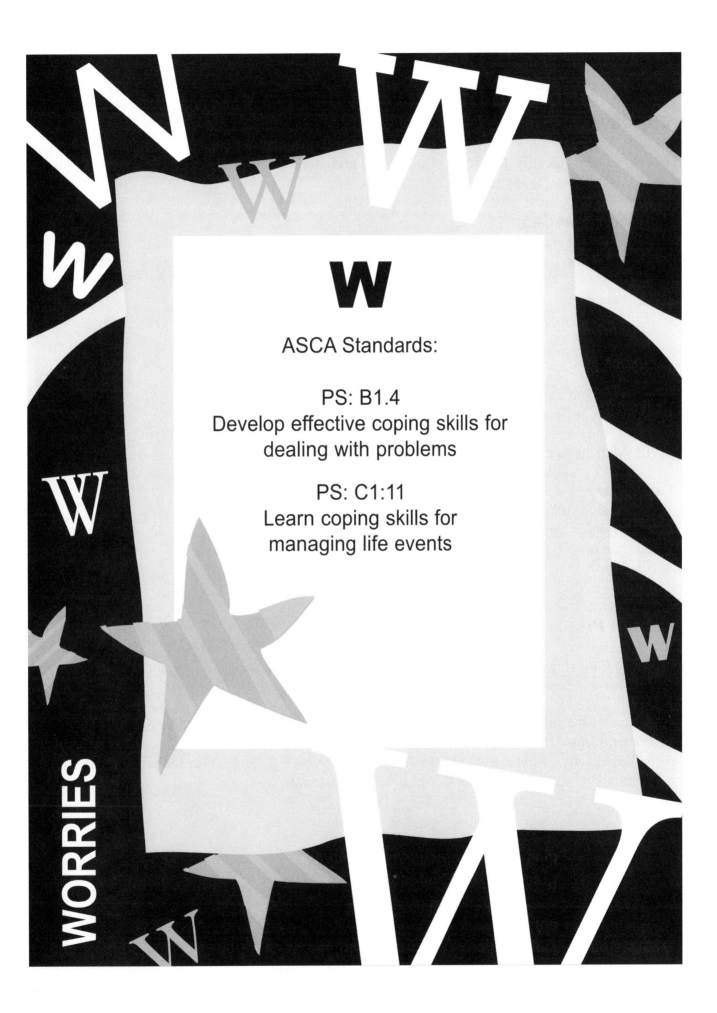

W

ASCA Standards:

PS: B1.4
Develop effective coping skills for
dealing with problems

PS: C1:11
Learn coping skills for
managing life events

WORRIES

WORRIES

Objective:

To help students identify the causes of *worry* and understand the effects of *worry*

Materials Needed:

For each student:
- ☐ Paper
- ☐ Pencil
- ☐ 2-3 sticky notes
- ☐ Yarn
- ☐ Scissors

For each student group (optional):
- ☐ 12" x 18" paper
- ☐ Pencil
- ☐ Markers or crayons

For the leader:
- ☐ Chalkboard and chalk or whiteboard and marker
- ☐ 17 paper bags
- ☐ Marker
- ☐ Tape

Lesson Preparation:

Write the following quote by Benjamin Franklin on the board: "Do not anticipate trouble or worry about what *may* happen. Keep in the sunlight."

Write one of the following common worries on each paper bag: *Grades, Home/Family, Friends/ Friendships, Peer Pressure, Money, Tests, Moving, Death, Pets, Jobs, World Situation, Illness, Injury, Physical Appearance, Change, Physical Danger, Other _____*. Tape the paper bags on the wall around the classroom. Gather the other needed materials.

Lesson:

▸ Ask the students to read the quote on the board and explain what it means to them.

▸ Tell the students there is an old proverb that says, "Worry never fixes anything." Ask if they agree or disagree with that statement.

▶ Explain that this lesson is about worries, the effects of worrying, and how to deal with worries.

▶ Have the students brainstorm things they worry about and write their suggestions on the board.

▶ Tell the students that 17 paper bags are situated around the room. A common adolescent worry is written on each bag. Talk about each one.

▶ Have the students take out a piece of paper and a pencil. Tell them to tear the paper into three strips. Explain that the class is going to make a list of its 10 top worries. Have the students pick out the three things they worry about most, write their biggest worry on one strip of paper, and then write three reasons why this worries them. They should write their second biggest worry on another strip of paper, followed by two reasons it worries them. Their third worry should be written on the third strip of paper, followed by one reason why they worry about this thing.

▶ Have the students drop their pieces of paper into the bag labeled with the worry that matches it. If their worry does not fit into one of the categories, they should drop their paper into the bag labeled *Other.*

▶ Divide the students into pairs. Give each pair a paper bag. Have each pair of students count the total number of points on the papers inside their bag, giving one point for each worry written on a strip of paper. Write that number on the bag and tape it back on the wall.

▶ Look at the totals to see the biggest worry of students in the class, the second biggest worry, and so on, until reaching the least-significant worry.

▶ Tell the students that there are many things they cannot change or control. In fact, 85-95% of the things people worry about cannot be changed! Since worrying about these things will not change anything, we need to try to let go of our worries.

▶ Ask the following question, then discuss each answer:

If you cannot change the situation and worrying will not help, what can you do? (*You can cope by changing how you feel about things.*)

▶ Explain how we can change our thoughts by saying:

- Changing your thoughts may help you let go of the worry. Positive thinking is a way to change your thoughts. Some examples of positive thinking are:

    - "I will make the best of the situation."
    - "This is out of my control, so I am not going to waste time and energy worrying about it."
    - "I accept that I can't change this, so I am not going to worry about it."

- Change your activity if you are feeling overwhelmed by worry. *(Have the students give examples.)*
- Try relaxation techniques.
- Use humor.

159

- Write down your worries and let them go.
- Talk with someone, then let go of the worry. *(Even though talking with someone doesn't change what you are worried about, it can make you feel better.)*

▶ Distribute two or three sticky notes to each student. Have the students write a way that worrying can affect a person on each note, then post the notes on the board. Review the answers aloud. *(Worry can cause: poor health such as ulcers, high blood pressure, anxiety, stomachaches, headaches; weight gain or loss; loss of hair; inability to work up to one's potential; safety issues; loss of sleep; depression; etc.)*

Reinforce the fact that worry can affect both health and performance.

▶ **Worry Warden Activity:** Tell the students they are each going to make a *Worry Warden*. A *Worry Warden* wards off worries.

Give each student some yarn and scissors and have him/her:

- Cut a piece of yarn long enough to wrap around his/her hand 20-30 times.
- Wrap the yarn around his/her hand 20-30 times.
- Slip the yarn off his/her hand and tie a small piece of yarn tightly around the middle of the yarn.
- Snip the top and bottom of the ends, where the yarn was wrapped around his/her hand.
- Pull the yarn so a pom pom forms.
- This is a *Worry Warden*.

Tell the students to watch their worries evaporate when the *Worry Warden* worries for them. All they have to do is tell their worries to the *Worry Warden* and let him worry for them.

Collect the scissors.

▶ **Optional Activity:** Divide the students into groups of four. One way to do this is to decide how many groups you need to have in order to have four students in each group. Then have the students count off by that number. If you will have seven groups, for example, have the students count off by sevens. Then have each student join the group that matches his/her number.

Give each group a piece of 12" x 18" paper, a pencil, and markers or crayons. Ask each group to make a wanted poster for *Wylie the Worrier*. The poster should list what worries Wylie has and the concerns the students have if he continues to worry and is not caught.

Have the students share their posters with the class.

Conclusion:

▶ Conclude the lesson by emphasizing that everyone worries. Remind the students that sometimes we can change the thing we are worried about, and sometimes we cannot. If we cannot change it, we should find a healthy replacement for it.

X

ASCA Standards:

PS: A1.2
Identifying values, attitudes, beliefs

EXPLORING
CHARACTER TRAITS

EXPLORING CHARACTER TRAITS

Objective:

To help students identify positive character traits

Materials Needed:

For each student:
- ☐ *Character Bookmark* (page 164)
- ☐ *Trait Bingo* (page 165)
- ☐ Pencil

For each student group:
- ☐ Paper
- ☐ Pencil

For the leader:
- ☐ Craft sticks equal to the number of students in the class.
- ☐ Blue, green, red, yellow, black, and purple markers
- ☐ Container
- ☐ Scissors
- ☐ *Trait Bingo Numbers* (page 166)

Lesson Preparation:

Divide the craft sticks, as evenly as possible, into six groups. Using a different color for each group, color the ends of the sticks blue, green, red, yellow, black, or purple. Place the craft sticks into the container. Reproduce and cut out a *Character Bookmark* for each student. Reproduce and cut out the *Trait Bingo Numbers*. Reproduce a *Trait Bingo* gameboard for each student.

Lesson:

▸ Tell the students that this lesson is about exploring traits that deal with positive character. Having positive character traits makes for a better society, promotes peace and harmony, and benefits persons who have them in many other ways. It is hoped that each student will develop positive character traits to benefit society as well as him/herself.

▸ Have each student choose a craft stick from the container and have all the students whose craft sticks are the same color form groups.

▸ Have one group member take out paper and a pencil. Assign each group the following:

Group #1 (blue)— a, b, c, d, e
Group #2 (green)— f, g, h, i
Group #3 (red)—j, k, l, m
Group #4 (yellow)— n, o, p, q
Group #5 (black)— r, s, t, u, v
Group #6 (purple)— w, x, y, z

▸ Tell the students to brainstorm character traits that begin with the letters assigned to their group. Make exceptions for *X*, *Y*, and any other letters you choose. Those groups may list character traits that include, rather than begin with, those letters. Have the students write their chosen character traits on the paper. The following examples may be used in addition to words named by the groups or as examples if the group cannot think of a word:

A—ambitious	B—brave	C—courageous
D—dependable	E—efficient	F—friendly
G—generous	H—honest	I—intelligent
J—just	K—kind	L—loyal
M—mannerly	N—nice	O—organized
P—polite	Q—quiet	R—responsible
S—sensitive	T—thoughtful	U—understanding
V—valiant	W—warm	X—excellent
Y—loyal	Z—zealous	

▸ Have each group share its answers with the class. Students in the class may add other traits to the list. As the traits are mentioned, discuss why each one is a positive character trait.

▸ Distribute a bookmark to each student and discuss the meaning of each character trait. Ask the students to name behaviors that exemplify each trait.

Conclusion:

▸ Conclude the lesson by distributing a *Trait Bingo* gameboard to each student. Tell the students to write a number in the circle inside each square. They are to choose from the numbers listed at the top of each column. Explain that you will call a number. Any student who has that number should raise his/her hand and, when called upon, read the statement aloud and answer it. Then he/she may cross out the number. The first person to cross out five numbers in a vertical, horizontal, or diagonal row wins the game.

CHARACTER BOOKMARKS

Caring
Honest
Ambitious
Responsible
Adaptable
Citizenship
Trustworthy
Efficient
Reliable

Caring
Honest
Ambitious
Responsible
Adaptable
Citizenship
Trustworthy
Efficient
Reliable

Caring
Honest
Ambitious
Responsible
Adaptable
Citizenship
Trustworthy
Efficient
Reliable

T R A I T — Character Traits Bingo

T #1 – #15	R #16 – #30	A #31 – #45	I #46 – #60	T #61 – #75
I was responsible when …	I showed courage when …	I was kind when …	I was honest when …	I was fair when …
My friend showed responsibility when …	My friend showed courage when …	My friend was kind when …	My friend was honest when …	My friend was fair when …
My best character trait is …	My friend's best character trait is …	FREE SPACE **BINGO**	My hero/idol's best character trait is …	A family member's best character trait is …
Our society would be better if people were more …	Our school would be better if students were more …	My family would be better if family members would …	My friendships would be better if …	The world would be better if people were …
I get along best with people who are …	I like to be around people who are …	A character trait that I admire is …	The most important character trait to me is …	Three character traits that describe me are …

165

TRAIT BINGO NUMBERS

1	2	3	4	5	6	7	8
9	10	11	12	13	14	15	16
17	18	19	20	21	22	23	24
25	26	27	28	29	30	31	32
33	34	35	36	37	38	39	40
41	42	43	44	45	46	47	48
49	50	51	52	53	54	55	56
57	58	59	60	61	62	63	64
65	66	67	68	69	70	71	72
73	74	75					

Y

ASCA Standards:

PS: A1:1
Develop positive attitudes toward self
as a unique and worthy person

YOU

Objective:

To help the students learn more about themselves and other members of the class

Materials Needed:

For each student:
- ☐ Sheet of paper and pencil (For Optional Activity)

For each student group:
- ☐ Die

For the leader:
- ☐ Craft sticks equal to the number of students in the class
- ☐ Blue, green, red, yellow, black, and purple markers
- ☐ Container
- ☐ Timer
- ☐ Thesaurus

Lesson Preparation:

Divide the craft sticks, as evenly as possible, into six groups. Using a different color for each group, color the ends of the sticks blue, green, red, yellow, black, or purple. Put the craft sticks into a container. Gather any other needed materials.

Lesson:

▸ Tell the students that this lesson's activities will help them learn more about themselves.

▸ Have each student choose a craft stick from the container. Have the students form groups with others whose sticks are the same color as theirs.

▸ Give each group a die. Explain that each person in the group is to roll the die, count the number of dots that are face-up, and tell the group members that number of things about him/herself. Demonstrate this for the class by throwing the die and telling the group one thing about yourself for each dot on the die. Tell the students they will be asked to remember one thing each group member says and relate it to the entire class.

▸ Have each person in each group tell the class one thing about another group member that he/she learned from this activity. *(Note: You may want to tell the students that they may not repeat anything another student has said.)*

▸ **Circle Within A Circle Activity:** Divide the class in half. Have half of the students stand in a circle and face outward. Have the rest of the students stand in a circle outside the first group of students and face inward, toward the students in the inner circle.

Tell the students that you are going to give them a subject to discuss. The students on the inside circle will talk first, for 30 seconds, about the topic. Time will then be called, and the students in the outside circle will talk for 30 seconds about the topic. Once each question has been discussed by each person, the students on the outside will take one step to the right and face a new person. A new topic will then be assigned, and the process will continue until everyone has had a chance to talk with everyone else at least once.

Suggested topics are:

- My favorite gift that I ever received
- My favorite place
- What I want to be when I am older
- What I like best about my friends
- My best trait
- If I were principal of this school, I would
- If I could visit anywhere, it would be
- If I could have lunch with anyone, I would choose
- What I would change about our town
- My wish for the world
- Something I would like to change about myself
- Something that makes me happy
- Something that I am proud of
- Three words that describe me
- The best thing that could happen
- If I had $500.00, I would

▸ Have the students return to their seats. Ask the students to share something they learned about someone else in the class. Remind the students that we are all unique individuals, and our uniqueness is what makes every one of us special.

▶ **Optional Activity:** Have each student write his/her name from top to bottom on a sheet of paper. Tell the students to think of a word that describes them and begins with each letter in their name. Have them write the word next to that letter in their name. Have a thesaurus available to help them think of adjectives that describe themselves.

An example for Maggie is:

Marvelous
Awesome
Generous
Genuine
Inquisitive
Easygoing

Display the students' work in the classroom.

Conclusion:

▶ Conclude the lesson by telling the students to appreciate how unique each of them is. It is important to learn about other people and accept them for who they are. It is also important for us to accept ourselves for who we are.

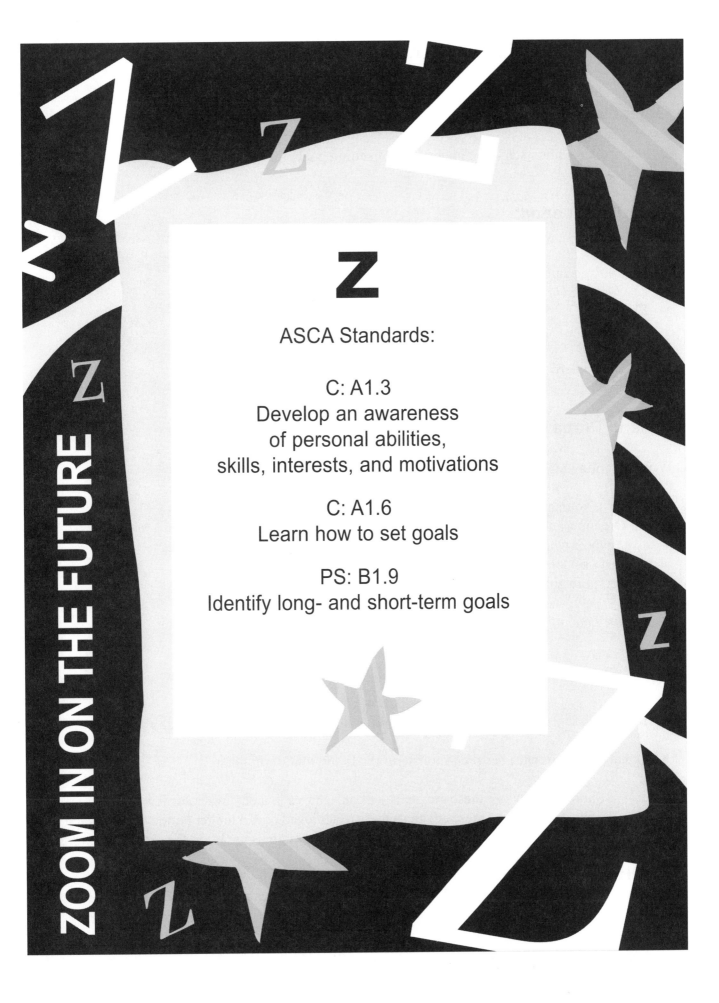

Z

ASCA Standards:

C: A1.3
Develop an awareness
of personal abilities,
skills, interests, and motivations

C: A1.6
Learn how to set goals

PS: B1.9
Identify long- and short-term goals

ZOOM IN ON THE FUTURE

ZOOM IN ON THE FUTURE

Objective:

To help students understand the importance of setting goals for the future

Materials Needed:

For each student:
- ☐ *Looking Into The Future* (page 175)
- ☐ *Zoom In On The Future* (page 176)
- ☐ Pencil

For the leader:
- ☐ Chalkboard and chalk or whiteboard and marker

Lesson Preparation:

Write the following chart on the board:

> **G**ive yourself direction. You are responsible for your life.
> **O**rganize and prioritize your goals.
> **A**nalyze whether the goal is realistic and attainable.
> **L**ist obstacles that may get in the way of reaching your goal.
> **S**et more goals, once you reach your goal.

Reproduce *Looking Into The Future* and *Zoom In On The Future* for each student.

Lesson:

▸ Tell the students that the topic of this lesson will be setting goals for the future.

▸ Explain the difference between short-term goals and long-term goals:

- Short-term goals—these are goals we can achieve in a day, week, or few months.
- Long-term goals—these are goals that are achieved over a longer period of time, such as a semester, a year, five years, or more. Long-term goals are often the most meaningful.

▸ Tell the students that this lesson will focus on long-term goals. As they talk about "zooming in on the future," they are going to look ahead and think about where they want to be in five or ten years.

▸ Give each student a copy of *Looking Into The Future*. Have each student write his/her name on the handle of the magnifying glass, then:

   1. Write one or two dreams he/she has for his/her future
   2. Write the name of the person or persons who will support his/her dreams
   3. Write some of the strengths that can make his/her dreams come true.

▸ Have the students share their completed worksheets with the person next to them. When everyone has finished, allow those who wish to do so to share their dreams with the class.

▸ Begin talking about setting goals to help the students make their dreams come true. Point to the formula for setting goals written on the board and discuss each letter.

   G   *Give yourself direction. You are responsible for your life.* It is important to know what direction you want to take and to be aware that the direction may change due to circumstances, interests, or things that are out of your control. If this happens, adjust your goals. Set new goals, if necessary.

   O   *Organize and prioritize your goals.* Ask yourself: "What is most important to me? What is least important?"

   A   *Analyze whether the goal is realistic and attainable.* If you do not make realistic and attainable goals, you may get discouraged and give up. An example of this is a person who cannot sing making the goal of becoming a singer or a person who cannot stand the sight of blood making the goal of becoming a surgeon.

   L   *List obstacles that may get in the way of reaching your goal.* Know what obstacles you may encounter and take steps to avoid them, get around them, or overcome them.

   S   *Set more goals, once you reach your goal.* Review your goals regularly. Set deadlines, evaluate, make any necessary changes or adjustments. Once you reach a goal, set more goals.

▸ Let the students know that once they have a goal in mind for the future, it is important to plan for it and develop skills that will help them reach it. An example would be that a person who wants to go into the medical field should take high-level science courses in school, possibly shadow someone in that field, get a job in a hospital, or even do volunteer work. It is important for a person to take steps like these to reach his/her goal.

▸ Give each student a copy of *Zoom In On The Future*. Explain that the students are to:

   1. Write, at the top of the paper, a goal they would like to achieve in the future.
   2. List the steps that will help them attain this goal. Some examples may be classes they will take, working in the field, shadowing a person, talking with people who work in the field, etc. Tell them to write down anything that will help them reach their goal.

173

3. List obstacles that may get in the way of reaching their goal. Some examples of obstacles are: money for higher education, parents who don't support their goals, etc.
4. List ways to overcome the obstacles. Some examples of ways to overcome obstacles are: working, saving money for education or training, looking for scholarships and/or grants, looking for opportunities, surrounding themselves with people who support them and their goals, etc.
5. Select a date for reaching the goal.
6. Sign and date the worksheet.

▸ Tell the students to put the worksheet in a safe place and review it periodically.

Conclusion:

▸ Conclude the lesson by telling the students:

This is the time to begin thinking about the future. More times than not, things change, and adjustments have to be made with goals. Life situations often change, interests change, etc. and that is OK. Change and adjust goals, if necessary. Good luck as you *zoom in on the future*.

LOOKING INTO THE FUTURE

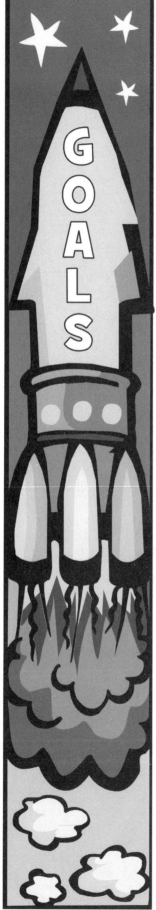

ZOOM IN ON THE FUTURE

One of my future goals is: _____

_____

Steps I need to take to reach that goal are: _____

_____

_____

_____

_____

Obstacles that may stand in my way are: _____

_____

_____

_____

_____

Ways that I can overcome these obstacles are: _____

_____

_____

_____

_____

I hope to accomplish this goal by _____

Signature _____ Date _____